READY?
The 3Rs of preparing your organization for the future

READY?
The 3Rs of preparing your organization for the future

Thomas W. Malnight
Tracey S. Keys
Kees van der Graaf

Strategy Dynamics Global SA

Paperback ISBN: 978-2-9700847-3-0

ISBN 978-2-9700847-3-0

9 782970 084730 >

CONTENTS

ACKNOWLEDGEMENTS

Embarking on a project to interview what started as 50 CEOs and senior executives around the world, and ended up as 156, requires support – a lot of support. Our first thanks must go to the executives who gave willing and freely of their time, experience, and candor. We can only apologize to the many assistants who helped us to set up the meetings and then fumed as our conversations overran. Thank you.

None of this would have been possible without the generous financial support of the Kristian Gerhard Jebsen Chair for Responsible Leadership at IMD, and also Kristian Jebsen, Chairman of Gearbulk Holding Limited, who has been a personal supporter throughout the work and offered insights and inspiration along the way. Additional funding to support this research was provided by IMD, and we wish to thank IMD for its ongoing support.

We must also offer thanks to our colleagues, who never questioned why we wanted to jet off around the world to talk to people about the future. They assumed we would find some interesting insights to share, not only in this book but in our classes moving forward – we hope we have. Again, we offer heartfelt thanks to those who made it happen – Marta Klincewicz and Cléa Estruch in particular, who never once complained about the challenges of rearranging flights and meetings last minute or spending hours on the phone across time zones. Thanks too to those colleagues who have allowed us to bounce half-formed ideas around and pushed our thinking even further; it has been a tremendous help.

We also received support from Kees' colleagues at Unilever in setting up the interviews around the world. If you have ever tried "cold calling" a CEO and asking for his or her time, you will know that having friends who can introduce you is invaluable.

Having insights and ideas to share is one thing. Translating these into a format where people actually want to read about them is another. We were delighted that Carly Chynoweth took on the challenge of managing not one but three voices in editing this book – and we obviously did not always agree – and worked her editing and style magic to help us reach the final product. Thanks too to the Strategy Dynamics Global team for their support: Lene M. Toubro for her diligent copy editing and Christel K. Stoklund for checking our facts and figures (again!). The book cover and layout is the work of Wendy Stephens at Dark Iris Design. In a world of connections, naturally we also needed a website, so thanks too to the team at Activate Media for their design and support in getting us online.

Last, and by no means least, the support of our families and friends has made this happen. For Tom, this effort, like much of the rest of his efforts, is aimed at contributing to turning over a better world to his wonderful children, Sophia, Alexia, and Lukas, as well as for the children of others. As educators, this is clearly our responsibility. For Tracey, her thanks go to Greg and Zander for all the support and encouragement, in the hopes that even in a small way this book may help us all find the future we need, want and can achieve together. For Kees, his gratefulness goes to his lovely wife Renée, for her support, and understanding. He also hopes that this book will contribute to the creation of a better world with new more sustainable business models. To all our families and friends, thank you for believing in us.

FOREWORD

by Paul Polman, CEO, Unilever

How we think about and do business needs to change. We need a more responsible form of capitalism.

The reason is clear. For too long we have lost sight of what the enlightened entrepreneurs of the past, people like William Lever, taught us about the right way to approach business and our responsibilities. Their form of capitalism lifted many out of poverty, gave access to education and health care, and improved the state of the world.

Today, we face a new series of challenges. The world is in the grip of economic volatility, political uncertainty, and environmental decay. Unless we act now, these challenges are in danger of overwhelming us.

We cannot rely on the politicians alone. The political system has not adjusted fast enough to an increasingly interdependent and more transparent world. Institutions have not adapted either, challenging the whole form of global governance. Today fewer political leaders are willing to confront the big issues or tell people the hard truths about anything difficult or controversial, because their timeframe is often guided by the next election. And in today's interdependent world, a lack of leadership in one place impacts many others. Think about the inability to solve the Eurozone crisis, or the failure to reach global agreements on climate change or world trade.

Europe and the U.S. are struggling to stimulate growth. Unemployment – and especially youth unemployment – remains unacceptably high, with negative implications for social cohesion. In many countries between a third and a half of all young people cannot find jobs. No wonder people warn of a "lost generation."

At the same we continue to push the limits of our planet. Growth has come at an enormous cost to our natural resources. According to the World Wildlife Fund (WWF), the developed world is already using the equivalent of one and half times the Earth's finite resources. These challenges to the sustainability of our planet will grow exponentially as we welcome another two billion people to this world and as many more aspire to higher standards of living.

Trust in governments to address these issues has plummeted and business doesn't fare much better. Even when many companies' intentions are clearly

5

to address pressing global issues such as environmental impact, a lack of trust means we have to work even harder to make a difference. Daily scandals, whether corruption charges, oil leaks, horse meat, tax payments or the fixing of Libor bank rates have done little to help. It amounts to an unholy alliance – a crisis of trust in those who lead us, combined with an escalation in the seriousness of global challenges. The result? People are taking matters increasingly into their own hands. Digital technology is allowing them to create large communities of interest, share information faster and drive action sooner. A billion and a half are on social networks and one in three is now connected globally.

Change is not coming fast enough for these new digitally empowered global citizens, so they are filling the leadership void themselves. They are driving the changes that others are unable to deliver. Think about movements like Earth Day, Occupy Wall Street and – most dramatically – the Arab Spring. It took just 17 days to bring down a government. Companies could fall in a matter of days – if not hours.

Companies that understand this and become part of the solution will have a bright future. Those that don't will be dinosaurs – outdated, outmoded, and out of business.

As business we need to start becoming part of the solution to today's challenges. Not just because it's time for business to be givers and not takers from the system that gives us life in the first place, but because the only way to guarantee long-term prosperity is to grow our businesses in line with the needs and aspirations of the communities we serve.

There is a huge opportunity for businesses that embrace this new model of responsible capitalism, but it does require a different approach. This goes well beyond CSR. It's about moving to a licence to lead, where business sees itself as part of society and not separate from it; where the focus is on the long term, not on quarterly earnings; and where the needs of citizens and communities carry the same weight as those of shareholders. It moves business well beyond the concept of shared value to one of shared responsibility – shared responsibility for developing more inclusive and equitable growth within the constraints of the planetary boundaries.

It is an approach we are pioneering at Unilever. We have given ourselves space to operate in the long-term interests of shareholders and stakeholders, not least by moving away from quarterly profit reporting and guidance. The Unilever Sustainable Living Plan, which is discussed later in this book, is guiding us – and our many stakeholders – on the journey to sustainable and equitable capitalism.

But even with our broad reach, we realize that we can't do it alone. Real transformational change will come from businesses, individuals, communities, and institutions acting together. So, if we fail to inspire others around the world to rethink business and what responsible capitalism means, then we will have failed. This is an opportunity business must not waste, not just because it would be immoral to do so, but because providing solutions to the challenges we face in areas like food security, access to drinking water, and poor sanitation is good for business. It fosters innovation and drives growth.

This is why this book is prescient. It's not another "Rework capitalism" book that sets out the problem but fails to help readers find solutions. This is a book with a purpose: to help every organization everywhere to prepare for a future which will be uncertain and volatile, but which also offers hope and opportunity.

I am honoured to be among the many leaders who have taken the time to share their hopes, their challenges, and their experiences in order to help others prepare for the better future that we all want. I don't have all the answers, and neither do they. But we are all embarking on our respective journeys with the confidence that what we will be doing in the future is something better — and probably very different — than what we did in the past.

It's a challenge, not just for the organizations involved, but also for each of us as leaders. Business has a much wider social purpose and value than just making money. It can and should be a real force for good. As leaders we need to promote that message — and so does the next generation of leaders. They too need to be inspired and involved in the journey. I am optimistic because I believe young managers today understand the need for change and sustainable living in a way that older generations, brought up during a time of abundance, don't always see.

The debate on the future of capitalism is well underway. I welcome that — and I welcome the important contribution that this book makes. Drawing on their own unique combination of experience, the authors have skilfully woven together a series of ideas, insights — and inspiration — that we can all apply to our individual journeys. This book should motivate today's leaders to rethink, redefine, and reshape their business and the way they lead. That way, we can prepare ourselves, and our organizations, for what I believe can still be an exciting and prosperous future for all.

Paul Polman
CEO, Unilever

PREFACE

Between us we have spent decades working as business teachers, consultants, and executives. In that time the world has changed enormously, in all sorts of exciting ways – and, of course, it continues to do so.

But the strange and worrying thing – the realization that led to this book – is that business leadership is not changing in parallel with this. Too many executives are only interested in answers, not in understanding. They want to learn the formula for immediate success, and then apply it, even if the formula is obsolete, or soon will be. Not enough leaders think about what might be different in five or ten years' time, let alone act on those thoughts: leadership today is all about today.

But organizations that are not prepared for the future will not last, so we decided it was time to press leaders on just what they are doing to get ready for it. We asked people running some of the most successful and fastest-growing organizations around the world what they were doing to ensure that their companies would still be successful five, ten, or more years down the line. If they tried to tell us what they were doing to hit targets or impress the markets today, we politely explained that we weren't interested in any of that. That's the bit good leaders already know how to get right. Our focus is what they expect to happen next – and what they are doing about it.

Between them, our interviewees represented a broad spread of industries, geographies, organizational sizes, and ownership models. Some of these companies and executives we knew from our work with them, many we knew only by reputation. We probed all of them on their successes, and their failures, and we are grateful for the openness they offered in return.

This book is the result of those conversations. It does not offer easy answers – there are no easy answers – but we hope that the insights and suggestions it contains will help leaders position themselves and their businesses to take advantage of the exciting possibilities created by the future.

Tom Malnight
Tracey Keys
Kees van der Graaf

May 2013

INTRODUCTION: GET READY

The future is a world of dramatic opportunity – and challenge. Technology is changing the way people live, work, and shop. Economic and social changes are altering the balance of power between developed and high-growth markets, with millions of new consumers – and a significant number of ambitious businesses – emerging. Even the very serious challenges ahead, such as resource shortages and environmental threats, also bring with them opportunities for creative solutions.

The questions these changes raise for business leaders are superficially quite simple: What are the biggest challenges and opportunities facing you and your organization five years in to the future? And what actions are you taking today to ensure that you are prepared for them?

We put exactly these questions to 156 CEOs and other senior leaders from a variety of businesses, including some of the world's largest and most successful companies. The men and women we interviewed came from different geographies and industries, and led businesses of all sorts of sizes and ownership structures. A research overview at the end of this book provides more information about the firms surveyed.

While the questions were simple, the answers we received were anything but superficial. In fact, we were struck from the outset by just how eager people were to discuss these issues. Many interviews started with the leader saying something along the lines of "Can we get this done fast, I'm busy," but continued well beyond our allotted 90-minute slot. Why? Because most leaders want and need the space to think about the future, and how they are preparing for it. They know that the world is changing, and they know that the old ways of working will not help them to answer the challenges ahead.

Knowing that they must change, however, is not the same as knowing what those changes should be, or how to make them. Nor does recognizing the enormous importance of being ready for the future remove the pressure to perform today; even the most forward-looking business people can work for people or institutions who demand quarterly, monthly, or even weekly financial results. Interviews often quickly turned into deep conversations.

The only constant ahead is change

The first question we asked was designed to uncover what leaders are expecting of the future, and how they believe the changes will affect their own organizations, and themselves as leaders. Our aim was to identify where business leaders expect to find the biggest opportunities and challenges five or more years into the future, and which areas are the major sources of concern.

These responses show a clear split between the views of leaders based in mature, slower-growth markets, mainly the U.S. and Europe, and from those based in high-growth markets such as China, India, Brazil, Indonesia, Singapore, South Africa, Vietnam, Mexico and Thailand. Leaders from developed markets, where growth has been slow or stagnant for some time, felt that many of the changes they were expecting would fundamentally challenge traditional businesses and ways of working. These executives spoke of commoditization of products, more demanding customers who expect to get everything for nothing, new low-cost competitors, and disruptive technologies upsetting the established apple-cart. Perennial issues such as finding, developing, and retaining talented people, building a positive reputation, and managing the effects of regulations also featured. When it came to opportunities, the more insightful leaders here spoke of unprecedented chances to reinvent their businesses and their organizations.

The view from those based in high-growth markets was rather different. These leaders still identified significant problem areas, such as issues associated with building the required social, political, and economic infrastructures needed to support the development of domestic market opportunities. But in nearly every case, interviewees' answers emphasized possibility and opportunity, not difficulty. Among the more forward-looking leaders here we observed a very strong focus on the need to benefit society as well as shareholders, not simply because it was the ethically right thing to do, but because helping to build stronger communities will help businesses overcome some of the challenges they identified. For example, some companies that are worried about a shortage of qualified candidates are responding by setting up schools or otherwise supporting education in their communities. That said, there were also leaders focused on exploiting their current positions only to increase their own personal wealth.

Despite these broad differences, there was one theme identified by almost every executive to whom we spoke, but summarized particularly clearly by Harish Manwani, the COO of Unilever: one of the biggest challenges ahead is not any one specific change, but the ever-increasing speed of change itself. "I think there is an increasing reality everywhere in the world that the only constant [now] is change," he told us. "The pace of change is getting faster and is often unpredictable. The days of long-term planning and predicting the future simply on the basis of the past are gone. The most important challenge for businesses is to create a point of view about the future and, at the same time, manage the short term more dynamically than ever before." Clearly, the notion of constant change has been around for millennia, and it remains a challenge today, perhaps more than ever, as change now is often disruptive rather than incremental.

Are you ready?

Anticipating change is important, but knowledge is not, by itself, enough. Most leaders have all the data they could possibly want about how the world is changing – if not more. The challenge for individual leaders is not letting this data overwhelm them, but instead finding a way to use it to move from information to understanding, and then to develop insights about what these changes mean for them and their organizations. That's why, when interviewees finished telling us what they expected the future to look like, we asked them what they were doing about it today. After all, businesses change slowly; if they wanted to be ready for the future, they needed to start preparing now.

Executives' answers to this question tended to demonstrate one of two almost diametrically opposed perspectives. On one side was a group of people who focused on the way in which changes to come will threaten their existing products, services, and ways of working. Their attitude can perhaps best be characterized as holding on to the past: they were expecting to continue to operate as they had always done, hoping either that what worked in the past would continue to work in the future, changes notwithstanding, or maybe that they personally would have retired or otherwise moved on before the changes became critical. In most cases these leaders did not deny that the future would be different from the present; they simply did not feel the need to do anything in response to these potential differences.

These executives, many of whom were based in developed markets, tended to talk about securing low single digit growth rates, finding consolidation opportunities, leveraging existing approaches in changing markets, and improving efficiency. They often described the necessity of "making tough calls"; many expected restructures and mergers to play a big part in their organization's future. They were always much more interested in immediate results than in preparing for long-term success.

The other perspective came from executives based in both developed and high-growth markets. These men and women were excited about what they believe the future will bring, and were making a focused effort to ready themselves and their organizations to make the most of it. For example, we talked to the CEO of an Indian business who had increased his company's market capitalization by 35 times in the past decade, and planned to grow it to ten times its current size in the next ten years. Another Asian CEO told us: "If we don't double our size every two to three years, we will soon become irrelevant."

Examples of developed-market companies doing inspiring work in this area include Nestlé, which is preparing for the future by transforming itself from being a food and drink company to a personal wellbeing company; and Royal DSM, the materials and life sciences company that began life 110 years ago as a coal mining business, and has since reshaped itself a number of times in response to changing demands. Look also at Unilever, which is taking a radical and holistic approach to reinventing its business to reflect the needs of society – and influencing those around it to do the same.

While some leaders in this second group spoke of taking advantage of high market growth rates, others spoke of genuinely reinventing themselves, of moving beyond past decisions, sunk costs, and traditional ways of working to find a new approach to business that would allow them to meet the challenges, and grasp the opportunities, that they know lie ahead. Unlike those in the first group, who were desperate to hold on to the past, these men and women were determined to own the future, and they knew that they had to start doing it today.

These people looked beyond immediate results and short-term success to the legacy that they can leave generations to come. They understood that in a few years' time no one will remember whether or not they met their quarterly sales targets; they wanted to leave behind strong, sustainable institutions that are prepared for whatever is to come.

Step up to the 3Rs challenge

We've written this book to support, challenge, and guide leaders – and aspiring leaders – as they prepare themselves and their organizations for the future, today. It does not provide simplistic answers or formulas for guaranteed success. Instead, we have distilled the wisdom of the men and women we interviewed, and examined some of the areas in which they are still struggling.

Each chapter includes case studies and perspectives from the front line, which offer personal insights from some of the people with whom we spoke, as well as a series of questions that reflect the critical issues facing all leaders today. The answers may not be immediately clear, but the process of asking the questions will move organizations forward in their preparations for the future. The "measure your progress" tools at the end of each chapter are designed to help leaders understand where they are in each part of the journey.

We begin by outlining the challenge facing almost every leader today: bridging the gap between short-term demands and long-term pressures. Preparing for the future would be hard enough if that was all there was to worry about, but the reality is that leaders today live in a world of two extremes. Most recognize, at least to some degree, that they need to make long-term fundamental changes to achieve long-term, sustainable success. At the same time, they are under intense pressure to deliver financial results today; pressure that can be so overwhelming that they have neither the time, nor the energy, to tackle long-term issues as well. And, very often, the most straightforward solution to one set of pressures can appear to make things worse for the other. In other cases, initiatives that are ostensibly designed to build long-term success are based entirely on short-term thinking, meaning that they are making things worse by lulling executives into a false sense of security without improving anything. Working out how to bridge this gap is a critical part of preparing for the future.

Then we move on to the 3Rs of getting ready for the future. Even the most brilliant scientists, creative engineers, and insightful novelists all start their careers the same way: by getting to grips with the 3Rs. Reading, writing, and arithmetic are the basic skills required of any person working in the knowledge economy, but they are also incredibly flexible tools that can be developed and refined throughout an individual's lifetime. Our 3Rs work in the same way: they are the building blocks of all that comes after, and they are tools that grow more powerful the more they are practiced.

The first R is Rethink. It requires leaders to take a fresh look at the world, observing the fundamental changes taking place in industries, geographic markets, organizations, and all the other critical elements that make up the expected future environment. It will help them to overcome preconceptions about what their organization can do, and help them to realize what it must do.

The second R is Redefine. We want leaders to ask themselves why their organization exists – that is, its purpose – and what their vision is for where they want it to be in the future. Redefining involves considering and making explicit choices on direction, including setting the ambition for the organization and the agenda for its leaders in moving forward.

The third R challenges leaders to Reshape how their organizations operate. Old business models, old ways of connecting, old ways of working: these will not be effective in the future. Leaders need to make fundamental changes here if they want to make the most of the opportunities available.

Finally, we look at how the 3Rs can help individual leaders prepare themselves for the future at the same time as they prepare their organizations. Almost all of our interviewees emphasized the demanding nature of leadership and the importance of having the right skills, experience, and mindset in order to bridge the gap between the demands of the present and the future.

One last, important point: we have presented the 3Rs as a sequence, but preparing for the future is not a linear process. Rather, it is a delicate balance of elements that need to be considered and adjusted simultaneously. And the future itself is not a defined end point, but a reminder that change is constant. Leaders cannot rethink, redefine, and reshape their business once, and count it ready; nor can they recalibrate their own leadership style once and leave it at that. Instead, think of the 3Rs as the foundation stones of a new mindset, just as the 3Rs of education are not discarded once first learned, but adapted and improved as the demands of the learner change.

ONE: Bridging the gap

Businesses today operate in two time frames: the immediate, and the very long term. The first demands that leaders deliver consistently strong quarterly results and keep their owners happy. If they don't do this, they're out.

The second requires them to make significant investments today so that the company is prepared for the future, even though these investments may not pay off for years, or even decades to come. If they don't do this, the company will likely eventually fail.

This creates an obvious dilemma for leaders. Devote yourself to hitting short-term goals and your job is secure but the company itself is not. Concentrate instead on making the fundamental changes needed for long-term success, and failing to maximize immediate returns will see you out of the door before your plans come to fruition. Try to do both and you will find yourself confronting the gap – the metaphorical distance between the goals, attitudes, and definitions of success that characterize each time frame.

It is this ever-widening gap which must be bridged if organizations are to succeed today and remain successful in the future.

Almost every one of the CEOs and senior business people we interviewed for this book mentioned the gap. After all, it is hardly a new phenomenon, with work on long-term business strategies dating back to the 1960s. Today businesses apply a host of tools and practices to balance short, medium, and long-term pressures, using approaches such as thinking in three time horizons of growth (popularized by McKinsey & Company more than ten years ago in *The Alchemy of Growth*[1]), and developing balanced scorecards (developed by Robert Kaplan and David Norton in a *Harvard Business Review* article[2]). What is new is the gap's rapid expansion and the increasingly compelling demands being made on each side of the divide.

The men and women we interviewed painted a picture of unrelenting pressure from shareholders and market analysts to deliver today: miss one set of

....

1   *The Alchemy of Growth*, Mehrdad Baghai, Stephen Coley and David White; Orion Business, London, UK 1999; Perseus Books, U.S., 1999.
2   "The Balanced Scorecard—Measures that Drive Performance", Robert S. Kaplan and David P. Norton, *Harvard Business Review*, January 1992.

financial targets and the company's share price can drop by 10% or more in a day. On the long-term side they described increasing pressure from high-growth markets and new industries crowding into their space, as well as demographic and social changes that are reshaping expectations of business.

Most leaders acknowledge that preparing for the future hurtling towards them will take more than incremental adjustments; that it will, in fact, require fundamental changes that take time to put in place. At the same time, it is clear that the vast majority consider making these changes less important than keeping on top of the things on the short-term side of the gap.

In a sense staying on the short-term side is the easy choice. It feels familiar, if not exactly safe. Executives tend to have a tried-and-tested toolkit of tactics and approaches that they are comfortable applying to day-to-day operations. They know how to stick to budgets, hit targets, and generally do what it takes to deliver short-term results.

Others choose the short-term side because they believe that it is their job to maximize returns to shareholders, not to sacrifice immediate financial results for possible long-term benefits. Cynical readers might even suggest that such executives plan to have moved on well before any long-term changes start to affect short-term returns, and thus have no incentive to worry about business sustainability in the years or decades ahead.

This explains why short-term thinking is dominant in most businesses today. Unfortunately, this dominance also means that far too many organizations are ignoring the threats – and the opportunities – that are building on the other side of the gap. And too many of those that are trying to deal with long-term issues are approaching them with a decidedly short-term mindset, which won't get them anywhere useful. Anyone who wants a reminder of just what such an approach can lead to needs only look at the Kodak story below.

So, sticking determinedly to the short-term side of the gap is a bad idea. Does this mean that leaders should leap across the gap to the other side? No – the answer is not that simple. Leaders who ignore the demands for immediate performance are unlikely to maintain the strong base that they need as a foundation for long-term success. Chances are they will also lose the trust of the people and markets making those short-term demands of them. At best this situation is likely to mean that they cannot obtain the investment needed to prepare their organization for the future; at worst, they will be fired or asked to resign.

The problem, then, is not short or long-term thinking per se, but executives' inability to deal with both of them at the same time. The key to uniting these two approaches into one focused agenda – what we call bridging the gap – is not ignoring their differences. Nor is it paying attention to one side of the gap and leaving the other to take care of itself, or using tools developed for one side on the other. Instead, leaders need to master the art of two-directional thinking, which we introduce at the end of this chapter and develop throughout this book. Two-directional thinking, thinking from today forward and from the future back, is essential to ultimately make it possible to prepare organizations for long-term success without threatening immediate performance. Paul Bulcke, the CEO of Nestlé, gave a succinct definition of what this looks like in operation: "We are long-term inspired, delivering in the short term."

Having a Kodak moment

Kodak used to be a corporate success story. For much of its existence it was held up as a grand example of what could be achieved by American innovation. Today, though, it is better known as a near-perfect example of what happens when a company is so determined to stick with business models that worked in the past that it fails to understand, or respond to, changes in the world around it.

For more than a century Kodak was admired as a model of modern business leadership. Its strengths included cost leadership, thanks to large-scale mass production; a strong global distribution base; a powerful international brand; and a commitment to knowing its customers. These strengths were underpinned by three key policies: fostering growth through continual investment in innovation, treating employees fairly, and reinvesting profits to build and grow the business. Few would find anything to quibble with in this traditional model.

In 1975, a Kodak engineer developed the first digital camera. The company got its patents in place, but failed to recognize what this new technology would ultimately mean for its business. As far as it was concerned, the strength and profitability of its core film business meant that it was fine to stick with its existing model: owning everything to do with photography as a hobby. "You press the button, we do the rest," its slogan promised customers.

It spent the next few decades fighting price wars with Fuji, its traditional film competitor, and losing to Polaroid in the battle for instant-print photos – apparently not noticing that its core product, film, was gradually becoming less and less important.

By the 1990s the rise of digital was becoming more obvious, and Kodak began to take a hybrid approach. It invested heavily in digital imaging, but also took a big bet on growing the traditional camera and film market in China, reckoning – incorrectly – that new hobbyists would want to start with film cameras before moving up to digital versions.

The results of this strategy lead to massive restructuring.

Next came a significant infrastructure investment in digital kiosks that customers could use to print digital images. This idea came straight from the "we must own it all" business model that had worked back when Kodak sold customers cameras, film to put in them, and prints of the shots they took. But optimism that the old approach would work in the new digital world was crushed by reality as consumers decided first that they could print their images themselves, then, later, that they did not want prints at all. Chinese photographers, meanwhile, made it clear that they had no interest in old technology by skipping straight to new digital cameras, bypassing film entirely.

In the 2000s the shift from film to digital became a landslide and a host of new competitors entered the market. Too late – long after Nikon, Sony and Canon – Kodak entered the game wholeheartedly, only to discover that it was much too late to make up lost ground. In January 2012 it filed for Chapter 11 bankruptcy protection; later that year it sold its digital imaging patents to a consortium of businesses, including Apple and Google, for US$525 million – considerably less than the US$2.6 billion it had targeted[3].

What can companies remaining in this industry expect in the years to come? The first thing to note is that it is changing faster now than ever before.

3   "Bankrupt Kodak Sells off Patents to Investors for $525m", bbc.co.uk, 19 December 2012.

Smartphones are becoming the camera of choice for many consumers looking to snap an image that they can share straight away on Facebook, Twitter, or any of a myriad of other social media platforms. Brands such as Samsung and Apple are moving to the front of the pack.

But the real point here is not that photography is a dynamic, fluid market. It is that business leaders in every sector need to understand that what happened to Kodak could happen to their industry, their business. It's time for all executives to ask themselves a simple question: What will it take to stop us having a Kodak moment?

The short-term trap, and why executives stay there

Short-term thinking dominates business because most leaders are convinced it is the only realistic approach to the world. It has trapped organizations and executives so effectively that only the most determined think that there is any point trying to escape it, which is why so few have started preparing their organizations for the future.

Those who want to should start by understanding why the trap exists – that is, the factors that promote short-term thinking. Most will find three main issues at play – financial market pressures, competitive pressures, and the executive comfort zone – while businesses operating in high-growth markets may also find that the sheer scale of the opportunities available to them has become a fourth pressure.

Escalating financial market pressures

Financial markets are one big source of short-term pressure on leaders. Anything that brings criticism from analysts is seen as a failure of leadership, while reaching or exceeding market expectations is cause for praise. This is why it is incredibly common to hear executives and investors argue that business leaders' sole responsibility is to maximize shareholder and owners' returns.

Not everyone holds this position – some countries, and the occasional company, insist that executives are responsible to all their stakeholders, with varying degrees of effectiveness – but it is a powerful source of strain on very many leaders. It also does much to discourage senior executives from the long-term thinking needed to prepare their organization for the future, by telling them explicitly that it is not their job.

One former CEO put this succinctly, if depressingly: shareholders want immediate results, not a vague promise of future benefits, so long-term oriented CEOs are unattractive. "The reality is that there is a cost to the shareholder of having a long-term [oriented] CEO," he said. "Shareholders are not generally interested in long-term benefits. CEOs have to produce their results on a quarterly and half-yearly basis. And they have to see from the market where they stand.

"The CEO with a long-term vision who is doing this may well be right in investing in the future. He may be right, but he may also be wrong. Nothing may come of it. And even if something does come of it, it may not come quickly enough to satisfy his own shareholders. The issue is that his quarterly results are being compared against others who are focusing on delivering today."

Combine this attitude with the volatility and uncertainty that face many businesses today and it is easy to see why a nervous executive might choose to take the "safe" route of aiming only at near-term targets. After all, such targets are both less likely to move and easier to see than anything in the more distant future.

But the logic of our determinedly short-term CEO has other implications, too. It suggests that many shareholders have no interest in whether or not the companies they invest in are successful in the long term. That is, the people and institutions who own these businesses do not care whether or not they survive the next year as long as they deliver the return expected this quarter. After all, shares are easy to sell. In many cases owners' profits come simply from day-to-day movements in a company's share price – surely the very definition of a short-term mindset.

Short-term traders can have a big effect on a company's market value, but they do not give two hoots about whether or not an organization is prepared for the future, because they have no plans to own it then. They care only for the profits they can secure in the immediate future, and act accordingly. Indeed, in some cases the financial models on which they rely mean that they simply want price volatility in either direction. For these investors, owning shares in a company is the same as owning any commodity or financial instrument; the underlying assets, including the employees and other stakeholders, simply don't matter.

Unsurprisingly, the growing power of owners who are in fact short-term traders or speculators worries business leaders who do want to escape the short-term trap. "Players in the financial community used to recognize their role as being the oil that lubricates and enables the economic engine," one CEO told us. "Too often today they view themselves as the engine itself."

This is not to say that all investors ignore the long term. Some choose to make long-term commitments to businesses in a way that aligns their interests with those of the company and its leaders. Warren Buffett summarized the difference in a talk to IMD's MBA Class of 2008: "They invest to exit," he said. "I invest to own."

One of the clearest ways to see the effect financial markets have on executives' thinking is to look at what happens in family-owned or partner-owned businesses. Here, where short-term traders have no involvement, long-term planning tends to be a more regular part of leadership. In many family businesses, for example, it is usual for executives to have direct discussions with the owners about how the company will be successful for generations to come. Partnerships, too, tend to be led by men and women who think about their firm's long-term success. Funnily enough this pattern holds true even in private equity partnerships that take a short-term approach to the companies in which they invest.

A handful of leaders of publicly-traded companies have recognized this difference and are beginning to think that maximizing shareholder returns should not be their only objective. They are starting to think about who their owners are, what motivates them, and whether those motivations are aligned with the long-term interests of the business. Some are even beginning to argue that part of their job is attracting owners who want long-term investments – presumably Warren Buffett's phone never stops ringing.

Choosing your owners is not easy, particularly for the leaders of listed businesses, but those who manage will end up with supporters who will help them to escape the short-term trap. Or, at the very least, will not try to keep them in it.

Exploding competitive pressures

Competition is a tricky factor to get to grips with in this context. For a start, it comes from both sides of the gap at once. In the next chapter we look in much more detail at the changing shape of competition and what can be done to meet it over the long term.

But competition is a particularly intense source of short-term pressure that can amplify the effects of the financial strain mentioned above, particularly when it leads to deterioration in short-term financial performance. Most businesses today are facing rising pressure from commoditization of products and services. Most businesses today are facing new threats from low-cost competitors. Most businesses today are facing consumers who demand more and more, but are not willing to pay extra for it. If you combine these with accelerating technological innovation, often leapfrogging traditional ways of working, slowing growth in many markets, and mounting cost pressures, the competitive environment is often tough, and getting tougher every day. These pressures threaten short-term performance and put extreme pressure on budgets, which in turn encourages many leaders to pay even more attention to hitting their immediate targets – even though dealing with this new playing field will require much more fundamental change.

Competition also has a more personal aspect for many leaders, who will have noticed that the average tenure of CEOs is shrinking. It's hard to tell whether short-term owners, impatient for quick results, are giving CEOs less time than ever to prove themselves or face replacement, or whether CEOs themselves are choosing to get in, get results, and get out in the shortest time possible. In all likelihood it is a combination of the two. Either way, short tenures combined with pressure from financial markets are an important element in the short-term trap.

The executive comfort zone

It would be easy to blame financiers and competition for everything that's going wrong in business today. It's even quite fashionable. However, it's not entirely their fault. Financial markets and competitive pressures are not the only reasons that short-term thinking dominates so many businesses.

As it turns out, leaders rather like focusing on the short-term.

Executives like answers, the more concrete and supported by hard data the better. They like taking action and being busy, not taking time out to think. They like results that let them show others that they are successful. This is what years of experience and their business-school qualifications have taught them to do. The short-term side of the gap is where their tools work. As far as they are concerned, they are not caught in a trap: they are in their comfort zone.

They don't want to bridge the gap because adding long-term thinking to their job just seems like more hard work.

"Business people find it quite hard to intellectualize or contextualize issues over a five to ten year period," Lord David Simon, the former CEO of BP, told us. "They're pretty good over three years, but moving beyond that is tough. But the issue today is that a lot of the changes that businesses need to make to be successful in a volatile environment take longer than three years to prepare. It takes time to create a shift of mindset, or to be open to new ways of doing things, or to build new capabilities. Despite this we still try to break everything down into three-year bites."

Lord Simon also noted that many executives try to solve problems by deciding their course of action then look for data that backs up their choice, rather than beginning with the facts and using them to find the right answer. "Businessmen don't spend enough time on ideas, the shaping of a problem," he told us. "They go for the solution pretty quickly, and then make it fit a set of ideas."

That's not just short-term thinking in action, it's lazy thinking.

Massive immediate opportunities

Senior leaders based in high-growth markets have one further pressure trying to keep them in the short term trap: opportunity. These markets offer individuals an almost overwhelming number of opportunities to get rich through speculation or by taking control of key assets or activities. Not all will put their personal wealth ahead of the longer-term development needs of their organization or their country, but the sheer scale of these opportunities means that those who do find that there is no need to look beyond the short term. They can expect to get very rich very fast, leading many to reckon that they will be wealthy enough to deal with whatever happens next even if they do not prepare for it now.

• •

Perspectives from the front line: the short-term trap

Vincent Mai The former chairman of AEA Investors told us: *"Often the fund managers are being measured on their performance, not even by quarter but by week and by month. So investors, along with the money-managers, are forced to take a much shorter-term view, which creates volatility. Short-termism is a vicious cycle: because investors are taking a much shorter-term view, it forces company managements to do the same. Therefore, often managements have to compromise, taking decisions that are not necessarily the right ones for the long-term future of the business. Unfortunately, that's the way the game is played, and I don't see a way to change it at the moment, at least in the public markets."*

Country head of a growth market from a major European multinational
"There is very little understanding or knowledge about what's really happening in the fast lane of the global economy, which is the East or the BRICS countries, at most corporate headquarters. In fact, surprisingly, the U.S. and European markets are out of sight for most people in these high-growth markets of the future. They are almost becoming irrelevant to where the future action will take place."

Ben Vree *"As companies grow their staff departments become more corporate,"* the former CEO of Smit International, a harbor services company, told us. *"This is a disaster, and you can see it happening. They start to behave in a corporate manner, no longer facilitating, supporting, and enabling the business; now they measure and control activities. They also no longer add value to operations, they now serve as a constraint."*

• •

Ask yourself: are we stuck in the short-term trap?

The short-term trap is insidious. It can sneak up on the most well-intentioned executives, as the pressures we describe above grow and demand an increasing share of attention. Constant vigilance is needed to avoid succumbing to the forces that would both lead you into the trap and keep you there.

Ask yourself:

Your agenda To what extent are financial markets and exploding competitive pressures shaping the agenda of your business today? Do the real needs of your business in preparing for the future feature at all? Do you have significant short-term opportunities, and are these dominating your thinking?

The executive comfort zone To what extent is it important to you to maintain traditional ways of working versus constantly challenging and re-inventing business models and ways of working to stay ahead of markets?

Assumptions Think about the assumptions that Kodak made. What are the assumptions you are making about your business and its environment in the future? Which of these assumptions do you need to challenge? For example, will your current business model win in new high growth markets and channels?

Do you believe you can control the speed of change in your markets?

Time Where are you – and your organization – spending your time today? Is it taken up almost entirely on short-term issues, or do you have a good balance between short and long-term issues? How much time do you really have to achieve the changes you will need to succeed in future?

• •

Forces for long-term change, and why they matter

Organizations and executives caught in the short-term trap are vulnerable. They are stuck in old ways of thinking, unable to change as the world changes around them, perhaps unable even to see those changes or appreciate their implications. Or maybe they have the opposite problem: they have so much information about these changes that it has overwhelmed them, leaving them unable to process it effectively or translate it into insights that will help them to prepare for the future.

Either way, the biggest danger of all these changes is speed. The issue isn't simply that things are changing, but that they are changing fast. Waiting to see what happens, or trying to respond with incremental adaptions as the changes start to hit, is not enough. Organizations that take this approach will fall further and further behind as change happens faster than they can react. Preparing for the future requires fundamental change, and fundamental change takes time.

Working out what those fundamental changes should be, and how to make them, is where the 3Rs covered in the rest of this book come in to play.

That said, we can't tell you how to make a crystal ball that will tell you what the future will look like. Instead, executives need to understand the forces that are shaping it so that they can understand what is most likely to happen in their own markets. Research conducted by two of this book's authors for the annual Global Trends Report identified a number of these forces, with the most critical being resources, organizations and communities, and shapers and influencers.

Resources: from abundance to scarcity

Not long ago the world – the rich world, at least – seemed to have an endless supply of the things it needed. Minerals, energy, food, labor, and the vast array of other resources on which we depend were abundant.

This is no longer the case. Today the defining characteristic of many resources is their increasing scarcity. As this scarcity bites, the competition for remaining resources will intensify, and may turn ugly.

Three resources likely to be the source of particularly challenging changes are people, natural resources, and time.

People The world's population is expected to grow from 7 billion today to 9 billion by 2050, with the majority of this population growth happening in Africa and Asia. The population as a whole is also becoming older, more urban, and more financially unequal.

By 2030, the world's largest middle-class population will be in the Asia Pacific region, suggesting that this area will be a center not just for low-cost production, but also for consumption and, quite probably, innovation.

Natural resources The changes in the world's population are putting an increasing strain on its natural resources. By the 2030s the demand for these resources is likely to be double the amount that the planet can supply, raising the risk of conflicts and other disasters as people and nations compete to control what is available.

Alternatively, and more optimistically, countries and consumers might find ways to adjust their demands so that they no longer take water, food, energy, and other vital resources for granted.

Time New technologies have taken over any number of dull activities once done by human workers, but despite this, "I don't have enough time to do everything" is a constant refrain in most people's lives. Information and communication technologies, which have become a central part of everyday life and work, have to take some of the blame for this. They provide a constant barrage of messages requiring real-time responses, with billions of people permanently on duty, multitasking wherever they are. Millions of individuals have found that the technology that was supposed to simplify life has done little more than add new demands.

For businesses, the speed of change and the rapid dissemination of information also mean that product lifecycles are shortening, and most companies are now working 24 hours a day, seven days a week just to keep up.

Organizations and communities: rapidly falling boundaries

Remember the days when there were neat divisions separating and structuring the world in which we lived and worked? Countries, markets, industries, businesses, consumers – each was separate and easily defined.

It's not the case today. The boundaries that let us order our world into clear, understandable boxes have started blurring, and will eventually disappear. Leaders will need to anticipate how these changes will reshape the landscape in which they operate, and adapt accordingly – something we cover in more detail in the next chapter.

Business The coming years will see the economic power of business increase. This is already well underway: in 2012, 40% of the world's largest economic entities, including countries, were corporations. Interestingly, this power growth is happening at the same time that trust in business is declining.

The way corporations work is also changing dramatically, with an explosion in the number operating as part of networks or partnerships that share resources, knowledge, and even production to meet the demands of customers and consumers.

Politics Trust in governments has fallen to new lows across the globe. More and more people are turning away from traditional politics and looking instead to communities of choice to get their voices heard. Over the last two years there has been a dramatic increase in the number who have gone on to turn these raised voices into action. The Arab Spring is one of the most internationally visible examples of this, but similar patterns can be seen across the world.

Alongside this, an inward focus on political transitions and economic challenges is fuelling partisan policies and nationalist sentiment around the world, creating the risk that rising geopolitical tensions could damage the global economy, and that separatist demands that could split nations.

Shapers and influencers: multipolar influence

Who can make people change their mind? Until fairly recently the power to shape and influence others' actions belonged to a relatively small group of individuals and institutions: parents, politicians, religious leaders, the mass media and so on.

Today the picture is very different. The shift from industrial to knowledge work, the rise of the empowered individual, and the rapid growth and influence of social media, combined with deteriorating trust in traditional institutions, is expanding the range of players who shape the world. These people and organizations can engage in fierce turf wars to maintain that influence, meaning that the challenge for leaders is not simply understanding who key shapers and influencers are, but also their relative power and importance.

NGOs There's a non-governmental organization for every issue, from tackling poverty in aging populations to improving girls' access to education and promoting environmentally friendly business. In fact, in most cases there are several – the number of NGOs is expanding rapidly. Most have one significant advantage over both business and government: people's trust.

Some can leverage this trust so successfully that they are becoming "super brands" with the ability to influence society both locally and globally. As a result, many other NGOs are also shifting their business models in response, for example by partnering with businesses and governments to increase their impact.

Financial power brokers "He who has the gold makes the rules," as the old saying has it. So, who has it today? The last decade has seen a variety of new financial power brokers emerge, including sovereign wealth funds, private equity firms, and the central banks of rapidly-emerging high-growth economies.

By 2010, this group had assets estimated to be worth more than US$14 trillion, giving them significant power to influence and shape future industrial, economic, and social development around the world. In the future they are likely to be joined by an even more diverse group of new players, from retailers to community banks to crowdfunding networks, suggesting that power will become more widely distributed across the financial system.

Social networks Social networks used to be niche websites that allowed people with specialist interests to keep in touch. That function still exists, but social media is now much, much bigger and far more central to people's lives.

It is now made up of a range of platforms that let individuals and institutions, including business, interact with all sorts of people. These platforms are already an effective tool for winning customers and employees, and have great potential for helping to create value inside organizations. The way these tools are used, internally and externally, is reshaping what companies do, what they make, and how they make it – co-creating products with customers is becoming more common, for example – as well as how they position themselves in the market.

The fight to control these interfaces and the power they represent extends well beyond the current leader, Facebook, to include other major corporations such as Google, Apple, and Amazon, as well as a host of innovative new businesses entering this space.

• •

Perspectives from the front line: the future

Harish Manwani The COO of Unilever is leading the company's dramatic success in high-growth markets. He told us that leaders need to manage dynamically if they want to bridge the gap. *"Today it's an 'and-and' agenda which says you have to have a long-term point of view and, at the same time, you have to manage your business here and now, dynamically. And you have to do both at the same time. The pace of change is so fast that what looks like a small isolated trend, or a niche, can actually overtake the world tomorrow. Whether it is internet technologies or social networking, this world is moving fast.*

"But the good news is that you can see this rapid change going on in some parts of the world, and you can pick up signals from there and, with experience, form a good view about the future. For me, leadership is all about having an informed point of view about the future.

"Where is the world heading? I believe the only way to get a glimpse of the future is to look around the world now, because the future is already being played out somewhere today, and sometimes we don't look hard enough."

Clara Gaymard The most critical skill for leaders of the future will be the ability to manage ambiguity, Gaymard, the president and CEO of GE France, told us. *"We have had a lot of people at GE looking at what it will take for leadership to be successful in the future,"* she said. *"The first thing that came out as the biggest quality required for future leadership is to be able to manage in ambiguity.*

"If you are not able to manage ambiguity, and you need to understand everything before you start doing anything, you narrow everything and reduce your options and possibilities. This will not work in the future.

"In a company like ours in the past if you were very focused – on technology, on productivity, on hiring and retaining the best people – you would be very confident about your future. This is not the case anymore. Of course we

need leaders who are able to be focused, but these leaders also have to have the ability to keep their eyes in other places."

. . . .

Ask yourself: can you spot the trends shaping your future?

In the future the world will have more people, fewer resources, and a much more interdependent way of doing business, while money and influence will be controlled by different groups and individuals. You as a leader need to understand which of these and other trends shaping the future will affect you, and your business.

Ask yourself:

Resources Who will own and control the resources that you will need in the future as they become scarcer? Have you considered all resources needed for long-term success, or just natural resources?

Society People today have more choices than ever before. Who is influencing how they make those choices? Who is shaping their expectations of business? How can companies deliver relevance, legitimacy, and value in a complex world?

Trust Who is defining and shaping the morals and ethics that will affect your consumers, your employees, and society at large? Trust in government and business is falling – who, then, can provide a moral compass for the world? What role will beliefs play in what your organization does and does not do?

Value Expect the notion of value itself to be redefined in the years to come. With that in mind, what will be commoditized? Who will be able to create and capture value? Who will win the fight to own the consumer – that is, to create, shape and control the overall experience?

More information about the forces shaping the future can be found in The Global Trends Report 2013, which is available online at www.globaltrends.com and from Amazon.

. . . .

Bridge the gap: invest in owning the future

As we noted earlier, we encountered two types of organizations: those holding onto the past, and those investing in owning the future. Their category directly reflects how they are approaching the gap. Those holding onto the past are stuck in the short-term trap, either denying that change is happening, or believing that incremental change will be enough to manage it. They often reassure themselves by focusing on the vast array of activities in which they are involved today – restructuring, acquisitions, leveraging existing products in new geographies, and so on – without recognizing that adhering to these comfortable, well-known approaches is part of what is holding them back.

Not all executives have their heads stuck in the short-term sand, and not all of those preparing for the long term are being shot at by their own side. Some organizations are led by men and women who are bridging the gap: they are actively investing in owning the future without losing sight of what it takes to be successful today.

These businesses tend to fall into one of two categories.

High-growth markets This category includes start-ups working in new industries in otherwise low-growth geographic markets, but most businesses in this category are based in the high-growth markets of BRICS and beyond (which we will call B&B for short), where rapid domestic growth means they have plenty of money to invest. These businesses tend to use it to improve their position in their home market while expanding into similar markets – that is, growth markets with a strong future ahead of them – in other B&B countries.

Very few B&B market leaders we met were interested in trying to break into stagnant, mature markets, because they did not offer the high growth that they were seeking. Their thinking often questioned why they should spend time and resources expanding in the mature, slow-growth, consolidated markets in Europe and the U.S. when the markets of the future were in their immediate neighborhood.

Business leaders in this group can afford to put less effort into bridging the gap, as operating in a high-growth market means they meet short-term goals almost effortlessly, while building platforms for the longer term.

Developed markets Firms based in developed markets face much stiffer challenges. They cannot rely on rapid domestic growth to fund investment in the future. Instead, their leaders must address the gap directly if they want to rethink, redefine, and reshape their company so that it is prepared for the future.

Some well-known leaders have started to do this. The leaders of Nestlé and DSM are both changing the fundamental nature of their companies' core business in response to changing markets, for example, as we will discuss later. Many more companies claim to be transforming themselves, although often the reality falls short of the words.

Here are two ideas for how to begin to bridge the gap.

Focus on root causes, not symptoms

We know that most organizations, and the executives leading them, are very busy. Most are grappling with an ever-expanding array of initiatives brought in to address a variety of short-term challenges. Many feel they barely have time to stay afloat, much less spend time on preparation. One CEO spoke for many when he told us: "Success for me is still existing as a business five years from now."

But firefighting will only get you so far. At some point, leaders need to start thinking about why the fires keep starting, and what they can do to prevent them. They need to step away from symptom management so that they can identify, and then remedy, the underlying cause of the problem.

If this seems obvious, well, yes, it is. Why isn't it happening? For much the same reason that many leaders like living on the short-term side of the gap: they know how to fight fires. They're good at it. They win praise for it. They are proud of their ability to pull a team together at short notice and put out fires that others consider unquenchable.

Fire prevention sounds a lot less exciting.

Leaders need to think about how they can reward people not simply for putting out fires – which is undoubtedly important – but for spotting risky areas ahead of time and avoiding them entirely. See "Two-directional thinking in action: Maersk Line" later in this chapter for an example of one leader who is determined to do this.

One CEO recommended "zero basing" as a way of identifying and remedying the real problems underlying business difficulties. "If we are confronted with a major issue we go back to zero," he told us. "We zero base everything and start from scratch with our thinking."

Zero basing means recognizing that if one approach has not worked, tinkering with it is unlikely to improve things. Instead, stop what's not working, look at the problem with fresh eyes, and find an approach that will. It means always having your eyes on winning the future, not on protecting sunk costs and past decisions.

Make time today to invest in the future: Tongaat Hulett

Executives under intense pressure to deliver today struggle to focus on preparing for the long term at the same time. Peter Staude, the CEO of Tongaat Hulett, has found a way around that problem.

The South African agricultural business operates in a region so rich with opportunity that deciding what to focus on, and at what stage, is a very real issue. Staude has faced this challenge by building a strong executive team that balances its activities across all the areas in which the business operates.

Most of the top and middle managers in each area – around 90% – spend their time working on issues that will directly affect profits. "We create aggressive targets in each budget area of the business plan, including expansion projects, that shape our day-to-day activities," Staude told us.

The remaining managers have more time available to focus on developing new paradigms, building relationships, working out how the business needs to change, and generally getting to grips with preparing for the future.

"You have these other, more difficult issues, where you actually don't need too many people, but you do need people with different skills," he said. "That's the other 10% of our people." When he started as CEO just over a decade ago, the proportion of people in the second group was more like 1%, he added.

"Let me give you an example of our progress. Our relationship with the South African government has evolved to the place where we are viewed as a corporate partner of choice in their land reform program. Initially, there was mistrust between both parties.

Tongaat Hulett has worked hard to develop their trust and now have a project – 3,500 hectares of new sugarcane in South Africa – where the government is financially supporting the project. We are working to establish a successful sugarcane growing community model in the deep rural areas of KwaZulu-Natal with black farmers.

"We can't include these activities in a budget because the issues go a little bit deeper than just putting roots down. This is where the 10% of our people focus their efforts.

"When you work in areas like this, you have to get your basics right first, and you then have to perform. However, you have to recognize that to win future marathons, to grasp future opportunities, you have to work constantly on these projects as part of your regular activities, both for risk mitigation and to develop long-term growth opportunities."

Embrace two-directional thinking

The challenge isn't just finding the time to think about how you can invest in the future: it's finding the right way to think. When it comes to bridging the gap, the only real option is two-directional thinking.

The first direction is the usual one: thinking from where you are in the present towards where you want to be in the future. Thinking in this direction ensures that short-term demands are taken into account, because they can be seen on the path ahead. It helps to identify what can be achieved with the business as it is.

Thinking from the second direction – something which must happen at the same time – means taking a view on what you think the future will hold, then imagining that you are where you will be (or want to be) in that future. From there it is a matter of looking back towards the present so that you can see what steps you needed to take to get there, given the changes you've identified happening around you along the way.

Being able to wield this dual perspective is one of the critical steps in breaking out of the short-term trap. It helps to overcome executives' tendency to discount all long-term planning on the basis that the future is too uncertain to predict. It does not provide a crystal ball – nothing can – but it can help to prevent leaders from making ambiguity an excuse for non-action. It is better to take a view on the future and turn out to be wrong than it is to do nothing at all.

Leaders will also find that working with others to develop that view will help them to develop important insights and unify the senior managers within their organization.

Two-directional thinking in action: Maersk Line

Paying too much attention to short-term goals is dangerous. Paying too little attention to the short term can also backfire. The trick is to find a middle way that allows you as a leader, and your organization, to balance these competing demands. Maersk Line, the largest container shipping company in the world, is doing a good job of making this work.

It operates in an industry with a poor track record of delivering value to shareholders, very high volatility in annual performance, and a less-than-optimistic outlook for the future. When Søren Skou took over as CEO in January 2012, the company was losing millions of U.S. dollars per day, and was facing the challenge of recovering from a huge loss in 2011. About the only consistent thing about Maersk's results was that it had not delivered value to its shareholders for a very long time.

Skou, working with his leadership team, recognized that the company had to improve profitability immediately. He also realized that he could not break the cycle of volatility without identifying and addressing its root causes.

His response was a three-stage agenda with overlapping phases. The first part, Back to Black, was all about short-term results. Its specific aim was to restore profitability within one year. At the time of writing Skou and his team have achieved the billion-dollar performance swing this requires.

The second part, Finish the Foundation, is designed to sort out the mass of initiatives taking place across the organization and unite them in a single solid foundation, and to make sure that all senior executives have what the company needs to succeed in the future. So far more than 40% of outstanding projects have been scrapped, and the leadership team has taken charge of defining what the company needs to do to be successful in the future.

The final part, Sustainable Profitable Growth, is about redefining, redesigning, and restructuring the organization for the future. It started with the leadership team debating the fundamental nature of the company – both what it was, and what it could be. They reflected on the changes that they could see taking place in their industry today, and those they expected in the future. They also considered what type of company the team wanted to build and leave behind for the future – that is, their legacy.

From this discussion, they defined and set long-term objectives and measures – both financial and non-financial – and identified and prioritized the must-win battles ahead of them. The leadership team now uses these battles, and not just discussions of historical performance, to shape its meetings. That is, they are thinking from where they want to be, not just where they are.

Coordinating these three agendas allowed the team to find the right balance. It was not an either-or approach, which allowed them to consider all issues, giving them the structure required to prevent one agenda overwhelming the others.

Find out more about must-win battles in Must-Win Battles: How to Win Them Again and Again (Peter Killing and Thomas Malnight with Tracey Keys, Prentice Hall, 2006), available from Prentice Hall, Amazon and other booksellers.

• •

Perspectives from the front line: investing in owning the future

Peter Borup *"There's a lot of protection of what we built in Europe,"* the head of Asia at Norden, the Danish shipping group (and currently president of Lauritzen Bulkers A/S), told us. *"We're protecting our dream now, and we're afraid that by giving just one concession that we're going to lose it all. But in Asia they're generally building their dreams, and many of them have very little to lose. That is a generalization, of course, but there is a dynamic and an energy that is driven by the hope and belief that tomorrow is going to better. It's almost tangible."*

Pat Davies *"What we're doing today was born out of a vision developed 10 years ago,"* the former CEO of Sasol told us as he prepared to retire. *"We are just witnessing the realization of it now. And if we didn't have that vision 10 years ago, I'm quite sure we wouldn't have been as successful as we are today. So it's creating a common purpose around a vision of the future that is key for us today. This is essential. Whoever takes my place is going to have to do this again if he or she wants to take the organization into the next phase.*

"We've grown rapidly but I believe we have the means to grow even more rapidly in the future. Growth is not a one-off job. It's about continually making sure you've got everyone on board and aligned and focused on the future."

Korsak Chairasmisak *"We have a lot of room to grow,"* the CEO of CP All, which operates Seven Eleven in Thailand, told us. *"I have a lot of confidence that we can grow from 6,000 outlets today to more than 10,000 in five years. But our future success is not based on the environment, which gives us the room to grow, but on the strength of our team and our organization. We have a very simple principle we follow. We focus on maximizing our strength, not our profit. We never want to maximize our profits. Rather we maximize our strength to optimize our profit. If we ever seek to maximize our profit we will destroy our organization."*

• •

Ask yourself: are you investing in owning the future?

The future is uncertain. The only thing we can be sure of is that it will look very different to today's business environment. Given this challenge, making the case for – and investment in – owning that uncertain future could be seen as a gamble, albeit an informed one. But it is not one that can be put off, because transforming your organization, as many of the men and women we interviewed are doing, takes time and a point of view on the future.

Ask yourself:

Root causes Do you spend more time fighting fires and treating symptoms than seeking and addressing root causes of the opportunities and challenges ahead? Where do you as a leader feel most comfortable? Have you challenged your assumptions about the business looking forward? What would it take to zero-base your thinking?

Two-directional thinking In which direction does your organization typically think: From today forward, or from the future back? Do most conversations about preparing your organization for the future focus on "What can we do, given our current resources and capabilities" or "What must we do to be successful in future"? What would you need to do to develop a balanced agenda reflecting two-directional thinking?

• •

Bridging the gap: recap

The short-term trap, and why executives stay there Short-term thinking dominates business today because leaders are under intense pressure from financial markets to deliver immediate results, and because they are familiar and comfortable with what it takes to do this. This makes it difficult for them to start making the long-term preparations needed to ready their organizations for the future.

Forces for long-term change, and why they matter Leaders need to understand how and why the world is changing if they are to prepare their organizations to operate successfully in the future. Key trends include resource scarcity, the collapse of boundaries between organizations, and the rise of new groups and individuals who can influence society.

Bridge the gap: invest in owning the future Businesses cannot afford to ignore short or long-term demands. Instead, they must find a way to balance delivery today with investment in owning the future. This requires focusing on root causes, not symptoms, as well as mastering the art of two-directional thinking.

Bridging the gap requires you as a leader to address four central challenges:

1. Recognize and manage the external pressures that could catch you in the short-term trap.

2. Recognize and manage the internal pressures and practices that could catch you in the short-term trap.

3. Identify and articulate the assumptions that you are making about your business, your strategy, your business model, and your mindset. Think about how these assumptions are shaping how you manage your business today, and how you will move it forward.

4. Find the right balance between short-term and long-term focus. Ensure that you are preparing for the future today, not holding on to the past for as long as you can.

Measure your progress

The assessment below will help you to understand where you are today, and how far you are from where you need to be. Key ideas introduced in this chapter are set out in the shaded rows of text. The numbered columns describe the different characteristics of progress for each, with 1 describing the least advanced and 5 describing the most advanced state of practice in companies today. Since companies may not neatly fit into one of the descriptions, you also have the option of choosing 2 or 4 as somewhere in between each state of practice.

We recommend that leaders go through this assessment twice: once answering from their organization's perspective, and once from their own personal position. We also suggest having others in your senior leadership team – as well as people lower down the organization, and even your broader stakeholders – complete the same test independently so that you can compare and contrast your responses, to gain additional insights.

Obviously, it could be tempting just to check box 5 and give yourself a pat on the back, but we would encourage you to be as honest and challenging as possible to derive real value from the exercise.

1	2	3	4	5
Effect of pressures for short-term thinking				
Our agenda is driven entirely by responses to short-term pressures and delivering short-term results; fire-fighting is our strength		We primarily deliver short-term results, but also engage with our owners/ boards in defining and shaping our long-term agenda		We effectively balance the need to address short-term issues with full engagement with all stakeholders in defining our long-term agenda
Need for fundamental long-term change				
Our business model and ways of working will be successful in the future and in new markets; we know what our customers need; we have lots of data		We innovate within existing markets and constantly renovate our business model and ways of working to keep pace with market developments; we have built insights about our future environment in existing markets		We focus on reshaping and leading long-term market evolution, constantly challenging and re-inventing business models and ways of working to stay ahead; our insights about the future have been translated into a point of view and actions
Focus of organizational time and resources				
100% of our focus is on results today		Our focus is primarily short term, with occasional focus on long-term issues		Our focus is balanced between short and long-term issues
Challenging assumptions that shape thinking and action				
Our assumptions are valid both today and for the future; we know what we are doing and what our markets want		We regularly review the assumptions we make, particularly in terms of our existing businesses		We constantly challenge our assumptions, and use scenarios and other tools to develop and evaluate options for the future
Our overall current reality				
We are holding onto the past; we are stuck on the short-term side of the gap		We have short and long-term objectives, but short-term performance is the primary focus across the organization		We are investing in owning the future, and growing dramatically today

TWO: Rethink Your Playing Field

It is impossible to prepare for the future without being willing to let go of the past. The only way to understand the new reality being formed around us is by observing and analyzing it on its own terms; leaders who try to use old ways of operating in the years to come will not succeed.

Rethinking your playing field isn't about thinking outside the box; it's about throwing away the boxes entirely.

Think back to what happened at Kodak. While its leaders gradually realized that digital technology could turn photography on its head, they did not seem to grasp that the company would have to make equally fundamental changes to stay competitive in the new world. They did not recognize that they would need to throw away the assumptions, business models, and mindsets that had made it a market leader in film photography so that they could build new models that would work with digital. They did not think about digital photography on its own terms. Instead, they tried to cram it into the boxes that they had always used.

Kodak's executives are not alone in their liking for neat, orderly, familiar boxes. Almost everyone divides the world in this way: geographies, organizations, suppliers and so on all have their own categories. Why? Because thinking about the world in limited chunks makes it easier to understand. Boxes allow us to simplify and structure our world. They help us to break down complex problems into manageable tasks and to define the knowledge and skills required to succeed within each category.

Take industry boxes as an example. We tend to assign companies to boxes by the products or services they supply: McDonald's is a fast-food business, Wal-Mart is a retailer, and HSBC is a financial services company. Once a firm has been allocated its box, we can see who its competitors are – the other companies that we have put in there with it. That is, other companies that look, act, and think like it does.

This makes the leader's job appear relatively simple. They know who to pay attention to (others in the same box) and they know how to compete to win within their traditional industries (focusing on metrics like market share). Thinking in boxes makes focusing straightforward: if something is in the same box as you, it matters. If it's not, it doesn't.

The problem is that boxes are wrong. Not because we've made them the wrong shape, or put companies in boxes where they do not belong, but because the very idea of the box is wrong.

Boundaries – those between industries, those between companies, those that differentiate between customer and colleague and competitor, and those between businesses and stakeholders, including society – are falling. Arm's length relationships are giving way to complex, connected ecosystems that are more like webs than a collection of boxes. As these webs and the connections that define them grow, they are changing the world in which business operates. Executives need to understand these changes on their own terms.

Playing fields are changing

The playing field in which companies operate is changing. So too are the players, their roles, and even the game itself. Leaders who continue to act as if the old rules apply will find themselves and their organizations sidelined at best, and left behind at worst. Old mindsets will need to be abandoned and replaced with a fresh approach based on what the world is becoming, not what it used to be.

This is why it is time to rethink your playing field.

Doing this requires leaders to take a fresh, clear-eyed look at the world around them. This should allow them to spot the trends shaping the future so that they can work out what they need to do to claim a place in it.

This sounds simple, but it's not. Executives' liking for boxes means that fresh eyes are difficult, if not impossible, to find. They define the world by what their company does now – the product it makes, the market it serves and so forth – and find it incredibly hard to put those definitions aside to take a genuinely open-minded look at what is changing.

One big challenge here is taking time away from the urgent demands of short-term goals to rethink the playing field not from where you are now, but by looking from the outside in. It means making your starting point for the future not what you do now, but what people will need and others will do in that future, and then understanding how your organization will need to change to meet those needs, and new roles.

This is the approach that Camargo Corrêa, one of Brazil's largest private conglomerates, is taking in its planning. "The world is rapidly changing, and we have to adjust," Vitor Hallack, the company's chairman, told us. "Our challenge as a company is to anticipate what markets will look like in the future and actively prepare ourselves for this future."

Your competitors are not who you think they are

Competition is changing. We don't mean that competition is becoming tougher, although it is, or that more and more of it is coming from companies based in high-growth economies, although that is also true.

What we mean is something far more fundamental: in the future, many of the greatest threats to established businesses will not come from their traditional competitors, but from companies in apparently unrelated fields. Any company still trying to fit the world into boxes is at severe risk of being blindsided by a newcomer from outside its frame of reference.

Outsiders can destroy your industry

Music is a good example of how this can happen. Until recently the fight for dominance was a competition between record labels. Each label tried to win that fight by working with the best artists and owning the content they created. Market leadership came down to sales.

Competition in the industry today — indeed, the industry itself — looks very different. Apple has entered the fray, but it is not focusing on content or the artists who create it. Instead, it wants to own consumers' mobile lives through the devices in their pockets; music is just one of a suite of different services it needs to offer to do this.

Then there are companies like YouTube and social networking sites. They're not interested in winning control of artists from record labels either. What they want to do is encourage consumers to think of music as something people can make and upload and share with friends online. As with Apple, music is just one aspect of what they are trying to do, which in this case is build and enable connected communities.

In a world of old-fashioned boxes, none of these other players are part of the music industry, which is how they were able to sneak up on record label executives who believed that boxes defined reality. Each type of competitor, whether content, pocket or lifestyle-focused, offers the consumer a choice of experience and makes money through radically different business models and mindsets. But from a consumer's point of view, this is the competition around music.

Banking is another industry that is starting to see incursions into its territory from new players. "It has already started but if you think five years out, the type of competition that increasingly worries me is that which will arise when much more banking is done using a cell phone," said Mike Brown, the CEO of Nedbank, one of the largest banks in South Africa. "The phone is not owned by the bank, and the customer is not now our customer, but the cell phone company's. How is the model between banks and cell phone companies eventually going to play out when more and more people are buying and paying for items on their cell phones using a mixture of mobile and traditional money? We are thinking very carefully today about how we position ourselves when this becomes the tool that people increasingly use to do their banking."

In addition to its own app suite, one of Nedbank's responses, launched in 2010, is the M-Pesa system — pesa being Swahili for money, and M standing for mobile — which allows users to download money on to their phone at any Nedbank or Vodacom outlet and then send it to other phones. The recipient can then withdraw the money as cash from a Nedbank ATM using only the codes that are sent to the phone — no card is necessary.

We found many industries with the same types of fundamental transformation underway, including mobile telephone companies trying to become lifestyle companies to take advantage of the connections they have already put in place, and retail companies preparing for a whole new world of where consumers will shop, and what they will expect while doing it.

What all of these cases have in common with each other, and with nearly all of the other examples of changing competition, is that traditional industry boxes are no longer part of the picture. Competition is now centered on what consumers want, need, and expect. It is customer desires, not companies' products or services that are shaping the playing fields of the future.

A buyer's market

Let's look at the emerging playing field of wellbeing and consider the challenges it is posing to executives as they rethink their businesses. Pharmaceutical companies will surely want to claim this territory, given their role in developing drugs to help sick patients. So too will hospitals, which treat those patients, and the insurance companies that help them to afford both drugs and treatment. Medical information companies, which provide individuals with knowledge that helps them learn about and assess their conditions, will also want to be part of it. And don't forget the health clubs and sports organizations which promote fitness and activity, or the food companies which focus on the health benefits of good nutrition, or even the cosmetic brands promoting their products' ability to help people look good and feel good.

All of these players are competing for consumer spending in this growing field. The issue facing each of them is twofold: they must start focusing on consumers' holistic needs rather than on selling their products, and they must recognize that their competitors are not just other companies that look, act, and think like they do. Competition and connections between industries is where the focus on growth and opportunity exist in the future.

The first time we made this point to the senior leadership team of a pharmaceutical business we worked with, they looked at us like we were from another planet. They were convinced that their job was treating sick people, and that their competitors were other pharmaceutical businesses. This is what they had always thought. This is how they had defined and looked at the world.

Much debate later, they came to see things from the consumer's point of view. They realized that their customers want to be healthy and well. They want treatment when they are ill, but they also want to avoid getting sick in the first place. Their customers are not just sick patients, they are individuals living full lives in which their disease is just one of many parts.

This rise of cross-industry competition does not mean that the future will be an unstructured free-for-all in which anyone producing any product is a potential competitor. Our point is simply that it will contain far more competitors than leaders will realize if they continue to think in boxes. The only way to identify them effectively is to stop focusing on your traditional industry and what your business has always done, and start thinking about the world from the consumer perspective.

Staying competitive demands connections

New competitors are far from the only changes in the competitive landscape. Companies that want to stay competitive also need to rethink what it takes to compete. Few, if any, have all the resources, knowledge, and products or services needed to shape and influence their playing field on their own. Instead, they will need to work with others – suppliers, non-profit organizations, government, and even competitors – to do it.

This approach is already proving its worth in some areas. Links between firms, individuals, and institutions are helping companies to keep in touch with the exploding pace of innovation by allowing them to tap in to a wider variety of resources than available in just one company. It's also faster and cheaper than trying to do all innovation in-house. We are also seeing connections begin to play a larger role in addressing global challenges. Climate change, food shortages, inequality, and other serious issues facing the world are driving an increasing number of partnerships between businesses and NGOs. In some cases these partnerships are fostering cooperation between competitors, for example in the shape of pre-competitive agreements to meet particular environmental standards, or to address the usage of critical resources to ensure their sustainability.

In other cases, new emerging industries are better created through partnerships between business and government. Take electric cars as an example. Customers won't buy electric vehicles unless they can charge them easily, and battery costs fall. Investing in the necessary infrastructure and in research and development is expensive, and could encourage car makers to keep focusing on petroleum-driven cars instead. This means that it may be necessary for the government to provide subsidies or other support during the early stages so that electric cars can compete with their fossil-fuel ancestors. But it's in their long-term interests – and those of the planet – to help reduce our dependence on gas and oil.

Making the most of new technologies, electric cars included, will take more from business than an analysis of costs, demands, and markets. It also means developing regulations, defining industry standards, even defining industries. This will be done by representatives from a variety of sectors and industries; if you are not part of these discussions, you will not be able to shape policy – and your own organization's business model – in a way that will allow you to be a major player for those industries. You are either at the table shaping the future, or you are outside waiting to play catch-up.

• •

Perspectives from the front line: connections

Frederico Curado *"Internally we have moved towards continuous improvement,"* the CEO of Embraer, the Brazilian aircraft manufacturer, told us. *"This is a never-ending process – more of a way of working. I am clearly devoted to this but I personally spend most of my time with customers, governments, stakeholders, analysts, potential partners, and other business associations. They are key to our future growth opportunities.*

"I do not believe that a CEO should always look more external than internal. I think the CEO must look at everything. The exact focus depends on what

the company needs at that particular point in time. But I think now, focusing on the years in front of us is becoming critical."

Brand Pretorius The former CEO of South Africa's largest motor retail group, McCarthy Motor Holdings, described the multiple challenges facing leaders and businesses: *"In South Africa we're facing a huge need for social development. There's an equally big need for economic development. We're dealing with a new generation coming along. Being a great leader requires contributing to all of these needs.*

"Our challenge as leaders is how we can set the best example to create a sustainable better life for all. This is not only the responsibility of government; it is the responsibility of each and every committed South African. We must reach out. We must do whatever we can to make the attainment of our national vision of a better reality for all."

Clara Gaymard The president and CEO of GE France argues that forging partnerships across sectors can help businesses shape how new playing fields develop, and can help companies to carve out roles for themselves within them.

"One thing that is very important for us is all the emerging new technologies – electric vehicles, wind energy, biomass, and so on. Often we can bring the technology and the products, but the overall shape of these industries is not yet fixed and the business model still needs to be built.

"In many of these cases the business model will be built in a public-private partnership. We have seen that in wind. We have seen that in solar. Unless you are at the table as these industries are being built, you will never be a major player in them in the future. You will at best be a commodity supplier of components.

"As a company, we must of course bring our part of the solutions, but we also have to be a key actor in the way the new business model will be developed and built."

• •

Ask yourself: have you identified your real competitors?

Rethinking competition is a critical component of preparing for the future. This means that you must take a clear-eyed look at the world rather than allowing your corporate history or traditional definitions to blinker your view; it also means being open to blurring the boundaries between competitor and collaborator.

Ask yourself:

Consumer needs Have you thought about your playing field from the perspective of customers and their needs, or do you define it according to old-fashioned industry boxes?

The players Who else will you find in this playing field? How do their value propositions differ from yours?

Connections What links these different players? How are they interdependent?

Shapers and influencers Who can affect your playing field without being directly involved in value creation? What capabilities does your organization need to play a significant role in shaping the playing field? What capabilities does it need to create and capture value in this new market space?

• •

Growth markets are changing

Developed markets, including North America and Europe, aren't dead, but they are far from vigorous. It has been clear for a number of years that it is the BRICS countries and other high-growth geographies that offer exciting opportunities for the future. That's why most companies based in Europe, North America, and other developed markets are eager to access them.

Unfortunately a lot of them are going about it the wrong way. The strategies of many developed market players today focus on driving efficiency and consolidation in developed markets, while investing heavily to leverage and promote their existing products and services in high-growth markets. In other words, they are all thinking like Kodak: not transforming their businesses to compete in the new playing field, but trying to use their old products and capabilities in the emerging new game.

This shortsighted approach is also reflected in their expectations, which tend to center on how growth in these new markets will help them to meet short-term targets, not on how it can help them to innovate, change, and prepare for long-term success.

Leaders who want to make the most of high-growth market opportunities need to overcome the dominance of short-term thinking so that they can understand the bigger picture and the full breadth of the possibilities in play. They should go well beyond identifying individual markets, instead considering the dynamics driving them; the models, strategies, and mindsets within them; and the economic, social, and political contexts in which they operate.

Power is shifting

Power is shifting away from the developed economies of North America, Europe, and industrialized East Asia to the BRICS and beyond (B&B).

The first challenge for leaders from the old triad is to stop thinking of these high-growth B&B markets as emerging markets, which can trick them into subconsciously minimizing or even dismissing them, despite their size and scale. These are growth markets with their own rules, demands, social and political environments, and strong, aggressive competitors.

The next is understanding why power is shifting towards these markets. Increasing financial power, resources, knowledge base, population, and consumer affluence are all factors. The global middle class will grow by an estimated 3 billion people in the next two decades, bringing it up to some 4.9 billion people with a combined spending power of about US$56 trillion by 2030. As the graph below shows, most of the projected additional spending will be seen in Asia Pacific.

Estimated spending by the global middle class

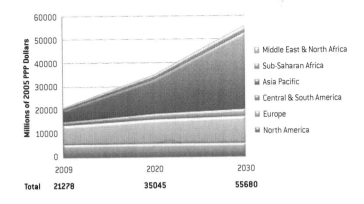

Source: OECD

The growth of the middle class is clear evidence that B&B countries are moving rapidly from being sources of cheap labor to the fastest-growing consumer markets businesses could hope for.

They no longer want scaled-down, cheaper versions of Western goods, but are instead setting their own trends. In fact, when it comes to luxury goods, B&B consumers are the ones driving growth. The leader of one high-end watch company told us: "We have two growth markets today. China, and Chinese tourists wherever they are travelling."

The rising power and influence of B&B markets does not mean that it is safe for businesses to ignore traditional developed markets. These economies are not the central drivers of wealth creation that they were in the 1980s, but they still dominate global consumption, and will do for decades to come. Once again, the challenge is bridging the gap: businesses cannot safely take an either-or approach, but must instead build an agenda that incorporates developed and high-growth markets.

It is also worth pointing out that demographic and wealth changes are only part of the picture. B&B markets are also seeing high levels of investment in physical and social infrastructure, which is increasing competition around the development and control of technologies such as high-speed transportation, clean technology, biotechnology, renewable energy, and space. B&B markets offer the potential to leapfrog older approaches and technologies looking to the future, thanks to their growth and investment.

Finally, the political aspects of B&B markets need to be taken into account. In each country the state will shape the business and social environments of the future, both within their own regions and more broadly. Competition between state control (China and Russia), chaotic democracy (India), social democracy (Brazil), and regulated democracy (Europe and North America) will set the environment for control of key future technologies and markets and, ultimately, the engines of future economic growth.

Life inside B&B markets

B&B players want to own the future.

How they plan to do this varies. Some are already strong competitors in developed markets as a result of their low-cost exports. Others are buying their way in, with Tata's 2008 acquisition of Jaguar Land Rover and Lenovo's purchase of IBM's PC business two of the best-known examples of aggressive investment.

But there are also many B&B leaders who have decided to sideline or avoid developed markets. They see little point in spending time and resources trying to enter these slow-growth markets when there is much more opportunity closer to home. Instead, they are using strong domestic positions and their experience operating in high-growth markets as the foundation for expansion into other high-growth economies.

Several Indian companies we spoke with are particularly interested in expanding into their local region and in building positions in Africa. Africa also appeals to Brazilian companies, as do other Latin American markets. In China, the typical pattern is to focus on domestic growth before pursuing global leadership, but when they do, Asia and Africa are often high on the agenda.

The consistent factor is the absolute focus on growth; companies have to double their business every two or three years just to stay relevant, the CEO of one large Asian multinational told us. This attitude stands in stark contrast to those of companies based in mature markets, where annual growth is more likely to be measured in low single digits.

So what does this mean for the fight to control the high-growth markets of the future? For a start, it changes the dynamic of competition within these regions, with the focus of competition shifting from developed market multinationals leveraging their business models and mindsets, to B&B businesses leveraging the high growth in their domestic markets to expand to other markets. B&B companies often have a closer connection to these other high-growth markets because of their similar backgrounds, market needs, business models, and mindsets.

The B&B leaders we spoke with often had a different mindset compared to their peers in developed-market companies — and one that is a better fit with high-growth markets. One leader of a large B&B conglomerate summarized the difference well: "I think our advantage is a combination of quick decision-making and organic growth opportunities, whereas many multinationals are constrained by their strategies and organizations, which depend on mergers and acquisitions for growth." There is a widespread sense among B&B leaders that multinationals underestimate both the scale of the opportunities available in B&B markets, and the work it will take to grasp them.

Partnering with a larger organization from abroad used to look attractive to many B&B players, but it has become something that many are now keen to avoid. These arrangements appear on the surface to offer benefits such as knowledge, access, and reach, but they also come with significant bureaucratic downsides.

One B&B leader told us: "The first thing you see is that the people who would control the business are sitting in Europe or North America. Understanding this business is hard enough when you sit here. If you are part of a multinational, you will be pressured to spend more time to help headquarters understand the situation.

"Often outsiders don't understand the complexity of our business. They think they understand the issue, but it looks a bit complex, so they get risk averse. And then they spend all their time trying to explain the situation, because it's so different from their own paradigms. Then headquarters gets nervous and it gets even worse."

10 x 10: The Godrej Group growth strategy

The Godrej Group, a consumer goods multinational based in India, has a broad reach and ambitious plans. It already operates in 20 countries in Asia, Africa, and South America, but its chairman has much more expansion in mind. "We are introducing what we call our 10x10 strategy, which means growing ten times in ten years," Godrej told us. "This means a compound annual growth rate of 27%... If we make it only to '8x10,' we will do that."

His strategy takes advantage of the natural fit between the group's businesses and the demands of many B&B markets. "We find that, because of the nature of the Indian economy, we have developed good solutions over the years for these markets by building on our main businesses in consumer products," he said. "Of course, we have other businesses, but our main focus is in branded consumer products that are suitable for, in C. K. Prahalad's words, 'the bottom of the pyramid' markets.[4] We find we can compete in the developing world because our products work quite well there.

"For example, while L'Oréal is the global leader in hair care, we are the leader in India, and in around 20 other countries in the world. And the markets where we are leading are all growth markets."

4   For more information, see C.K. Prahalad, *The Fortune at the Bottom of the Pyramid: Eradicating Poverty Through Profits*, Prentice Hall, 2006.

He has only the barest interest in developed markets. "We are clearly focused on the developing world; we are not interested in acquisitions in the developed world," he said. "We go where our products can be translated well, and that is not in the developed world where the overall growth is low.

We did acquire one company in England, which fit from a brand point of view with Indian consumers, but generally, we're interested in growth only in the developing world."

Perspectives from the front line: opportunities

Marcelo Odebrecht *"We focus on what the client needs, not what we can provide,"* Odebrecht, the group chairman of the large Brazilian conglomerate that bears his name, told us. *"If the client needs something that we have traditionally not done, our issue is to learn and deliver, therefore, dreaming the client's dream.*

"The government of a country in Africa or Latin America, for example, may not need someone to provide only infrastructure. They may need someone that can build and operate enterprises from supermarkets to hospitals and schools.

"One example is Venezuela, where we started as a construction company. We began a project near Colombia, and what began as a simple infrastructure project ended up focusing on how to prepare for and move thousands of people to a new place, which required building not only cities, but also farms and other facilities to enable the population to live in a sustainable way. This was based on our understanding that we could not focus only on construction, but rather on what the client needed."

Harish Manwani *"The opportunity is truly a generational one,"* Unilever's COO, who is also the chairman of Hindustan Lever, told us. *"The entire population growth and most economic growth is going to come from the developing world. It's a fact that developing markets, and specifically Asia, will shape the economic future of the world.*

"Until five years ago, people said China manufactured for the world, and the U.S. consumed to keep the world economy going. There is now a convergence between the consuming world and the supplying world. Increasingly, consumption is shifting to the developing markets. China is already the world's largest market for luxury goods, automobiles, mobile phones and many other products, and this shift is only just beginning."

• •

Winning a big slice of the market: The Pizza Company

New markets require new thinking, not the same old attitudes in different jargon. Multinationals that expand into B&B markets without recognizing this can find themselves struggling when business models developed for Europe or North America – high-income, low-growth markets – run in to models designed specifically for the low-income, high-growth markets in which they are now operating.

William Heinecke, the chairman and CEO of Minor International Plc., based in Thailand, has seen this happen. One of his group's operations is a restaurant franchise business. For 25 years this company ran the Pizza Hut franchise in Thailand, capturing 97% of the country's pizza restaurant market in the process.

In 2000, Pizza Hut took the local business back. "They owned the brand, and thought it was all about brands," Heinecke said. "So they built and operated stores of their own, and we started a new chain called The Pizza Company." Creating The Pizza Company brand was not easy. "It was a very messy situation. We had to show and prove that we were creating our own flavors and not using any of their recipes or trade secrets," he said.

What differentiated the Thai company from its megabrand competitor was the way it created its own recipes: by using the best research it could find about what Thai customers looked for in a tasty pizza. For example, Heinecke and his staff had noticed that Thai consumers liked more tomato sauce than Pizza Hut recipes called for. "Thailand is one of the few places that you will see a bottle of ketchup on the table in a Pizza Hut restaurant, because diners always like to add more sauce," he said.

"You're not going to tell Pizza Hut, the world leader in pizzas, that they have to change their formula for Thailand. They would say 'the Thais will adapt to the taste of pizza, as they adapt to the taste of Pepsi'."

As things turned out, consumers preferred ordering pizzas tailored to their tastes ahead of adapting their preferences, and The Pizza Company now has around 70% of the Thai market. It has used its success in Thailand as the base for expansion across Asia and into the Middle East. By 2009, the company operated outlets and franchises in Thailand, China, Cambodia, Saudi Arabia, the UAE, Bahrain, and Jordan.

Most multinationals assume that, as major global businesses, they know everything there is to know about their product category – making pizza, for example – and that no upstart local business would be able to compete with them. They also assume that a global brand and the standard business model that got them where they are today will be just as effective in new contexts.

In an era of strong multinational power and weak local competitive capabilities, this may have been the case.

It isn't any more.

Ask yourself: how will high-growth markets change your playing field?

Rethinking your playing field requires you to take an unbiased view of the competition and opportunities provided by high-growth markets, as well as the approaches needed to succeed there.

Ask yourself:

Big picture What role do B&B markets play in your overall strategy? How does this relate to short-term growth targets? How is it helping you to reinvent your company to deal with long-term macro-economic changes?

Balance How are you balancing expanding into the markets of the future with protecting or leveraging your existing core markets? How are you balancing leveraging existing products and business models with innovating new ones?

Barriers What are the major obstacles you face in preparing your organization to compete in an economic future led, or at least co-led, by B&B markets? Consider products, services, business models, and mindsets.

Change What will you need to do differently to serve these markets successfully? What new capabilities do you need to build? How will you manage different business models simultaneously?

Location What would be the implications of moving your headquarters to China, India, or Brazil to prepare your leaders and your businesses for the future?

• •

Consumers are changing

Consumers, and customers, are changing as fast as competition.

They expect companies to care. They want to interact with business in different ways. They want the chance to help design and make products, not just to buy them. Very often they do not want to pay more for these extras – they expect to get them free.

They are also, as we said earlier, absolutely central to understanding the new playing fields. Businesses must rethink their business around these changing customers, not their own traditional products, services, and mindsets.

Defined by diversity

There is no such thing as a typical consumer any more, if indeed there ever was. Consumers are becoming increasingly diverse, with those differences being marked not just between geographic markets, but within them. Companies need to develop and manage multiple business models simultaneously if they are to be able to meet consumers' many and varying demands.

Emerging markets provide the clearest example of this. The demands of the newly affluent middle class in these countries are driving massive innovation in products, services, and experiences. Many seek out luxury goods and high-status brands. It's also worth noting that by 2030 this group will have 2.6 times more spending power than they do today.

Then there are "bottom of the pyramid" customers in the same high-growth markets who do not have the middle class's expensive tastes, or wealth, but whose demands still present clear opportunities for the right business model.

Socioeconomic status is just one differentiator. Demographics have an equally important part to play as our population ages and multiple generations, each with very different experiences, behaviors, and expectations, share the world. Baby boomers and members of Generation X are gradually being overtaken by Generation Y and the ever more tech-savvy generations following in their digital footsteps.

For the moment, at least, the first two listed have the most money to spend, making them superficially the most important consumers. But companies ignore the younger generations at their peril. These generations are already having significant influence over consumers' behavior and consumption patterns; they are probably doing more to reshape this than any other group. Why? Because they have embraced digital attitudes in a way that permeates every facet of life and work. Social networking, cloud computing, and cyberspace – concepts that overwhelm many in older generations – are understood instinctively. Members of Generation Y are the first of the new digital cognoscenti who will guide the global population through the chaos, complexity, and intellectual overburden of early 21st century cyber-socialization.

If that sounds like too much for one generation, don't worry. In ten years' time Generation Z will consider them as antiquated as the rest of us.

The rise of consumer power

Consumers today are not simply more demanding than in the past; they are also more powerful than ever before.

Things were very different in the 1990s. Just twenty years ago most firms operated from bricks-and-mortar offices and sold physical objects that customers could take with them, or services that they could use either on the company's premises, or those of its distributors. Consumers, meanwhile, did just that – consume.

While this picture is a simplification, it helps to illustrate that the flow of business used to be relatively straightforward. Products and services moved along a fairly linear value chain, which was largely driven by producer companies and, to an extent, retail channels. Consumers' power was limited, as was their involvement in the creation of value. Their interaction with producers, brands, and retailers was typically one-way via broadcast and print media.

Similarly, technology was seen as a simple tool that allowed firms to keep track of their transactions and other records. Managing this data was a necessary chore, not a source of insight or innovation.

The internet changed all this. It drove increased dissemination of knowledge and transparency of information. It put new digital and mobile tools into consumers' hands, and gave them a simple way to talk back to business, and to talk about business with other consumers around the word.

In 2013, almost 40% of the world's population – more than 2.7 billion people – is online. A decade earlier only 12% was. Today, the mobile phone penetration rate stands at 96% globally, up from around 20% over the same period, according to statistics from the International Telecommunications Union.[5] Rates of mobile phone ownership have grown exponentially in both developed countries, where the 2013 penetration rate reached 128%, and in developing countries, where 89% of people had mobile phones.

In other words, most of the world can talk to, and share information with, the rest of the world. Technology has linked consumers, but the connections don't stop there. It is also fuelling new ways for businesses and their customers to interact and create value.

End-user customization may well consign mass consumption to the past, as more people decide that they want to choose the color and trim on their sneakers, as Nike allows, or select which parts of a digital newspaper they want on their tablet. Co-creation, which takes customization several steps further, is on the rise as more consumers demonstrate the awareness, interest, and ability to provide input throughout the design process.

Consumer involvement in business does not have to stop with product design. Business models, too, are being reshaped by consumers. Take crowdfunding, where consumers invest in a business or product so that it can be created and they can buy it. This and other crowd-led approaches can create organizations that blur the line between consumption and business.

PatientsLikeMe.com, an online health-based community, is a good example of this. It allows its 150,000 or so members to learn and share information about their conditions, treatment, and symptoms. The site does not allow advertising, instead basing its business model on aligning patient and industry interests. This means that patients get free access to a wealth of information and advice, while healthcare businesses can buy access to the site's (anonymous) data – which they can then use to develop better drugs, medical devices, and other treatments.

....

5   International Telecommunications Union fact sheet 2013.

The rising power of connected consumers will have a major effect on business. It means that firms will move from being the central players in a physical value chain to nodes in an open network of value creation that spans the physical and digital worlds.

In this connected world, no one organization can hope to meet all of its customers' needs alone. At the end of the day, there is only one common denominator: the power of the consumer.

Beyond the consumer to connected communities

So far we've been talking about the power of "the" consumer, but their real power comes from their multiple connections to other consumers. Business can no longer regard consumers as separate, self-determining entities. Each individual's links with others in their extended networks means that businesses are never talking with just one consumer, but with the multiple communities to which the consumer belongs.

This is a world where word of mouth and, increasingly, word of mouse, dominate the landscape. There is nothing new about people using their friends as sources of good advice. What is new is the size and scale on which technology has allowed this to take place.

Connected consumers are not just interested in talking about fashionable brands or interesting products. These are consumers who care. They want to know how benefits are being divided between individuals and corporations, and between business and society. They want to know how the products and services they buy affect the world around them. The pressure created by these demands, which are backed by high expectations of positive social impact, is shaping regulations, laws, morals, and behavior.

Connected consumers' desire to reward or punish companies according to their behavior makes it more important than ever for businesses to have strong corporate policies that will help to build public trust. Many are already integrating responsible, sustainable practices into their operations, and setting up partnerships with suppliers and other stakeholders to increase transparency, accountability, and credibility. Others are experimenting with social and mobile media to improve their communication with consumers and communities, although in most cases there is still a long way to go before they get it right.

Consumers want experiences, not commodities

Products become less interesting to consumers as they become more commoditized. Instead, they are seeking experiences that are relevant to their particular needs and desires.

Think back to our earlier example about the music industry. In that case, the nature of competition changed as consumers became less interested in buying records, CDs, and other physical products. What they actually wanted to buy was the experience of listening to and sharing music wherever they chose; in other words, music as a service that fitted into their connected mobile lifestyles, not a product that sat on a shelf.

This pattern plays out across other sectors, too. Consumers no longer buy mobile phones for the physical product, but because they allow them to tap into an ever-expanding array of services. Even television remote controls are now expected to control more than the box in the corner of the room.

Ordinary goods and services are no longer enough to attract and retain consumers. Nor is it only about receiving a tangible product or service: individualism and uniqueness are key. In an age of information overload, mass communication and advertising is tiresome – consumers demand personalized and relevant content and experiences. They are also more likely than ever to create and share their own content in the form of online reviews, user groups, fan (and critic) pages, and more.

The expanding role of influencers and gatekeepers

This ability for anyone to say anything, and then share it with others, means that leaders must take a fresh look at whose opinion can affect their business. Identifying the new shapers and influencers is critical, because these are the people and institutions changing the rules of engagement. How people share personal information and interact with others is changing as new behaviors and norms emerge from social networks, for example. Buying groups are tapping into the size of crowds to achieve new levels of price negotiation with businesses. Global reputations are made and destroyed in minutes as news flows through an ever-expanding range of channels.

People and organizations with influence used to be relatively easy to spot: the president of a nation, religious leaders, CEOs, and – often – people's parents. Their influence was based on a combination of position, experience, knowledge, wealth, and their control of the (limited) channels of communication to people at large.

This last factor is critical, because influence must spread if it is to have power. It is also one of the reasons why the people and groups with influence have changed in the last two decades.

Organizations that control the channels through which influence flows are now at the heart of things. Search engines, social networks, purchasing portals, and information aggregators such as Google, Facebook, and Baidu have become the new gatekeepers. They control the digital information stream and the new technologies that drive the different interfaces. This gives them the potential to have an enormous impact on how societies, values, politics, markets, consumers, and businesses develop in the future.

Businesses and consumers need to manage this growing array of channels and intermediaries. They need to have a clear idea how their information is being filtered, aggregated, and relayed to others – and who those others are. They also need to understand the intense battles going on for control of key interfaces.

The world of social business

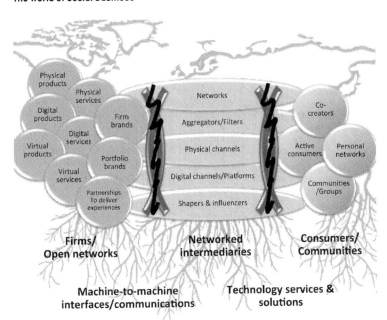

Source: The Global Trends Report 2013

Leaders also need to juggle simultaneous multiplayer relationships, including those between their firm and other organizations, and those between their firm and networks of communities, groups, and consumers, while dealing with the exploding number of different interfaces that allow them to do this. As you can see from the graphic, preparing for the future means working without straight lines.

Competing for the new consumer

So what does it take to compete in a world where consumers are connected, mobile, and more interested in experiences than products or services?

Two things, done simultaneously: enhancing consumers' willingness to pay by rethinking the value and features that your business offers; and enhancing their desire to engage with your business in a way that goes beyond a simple purchase. Together, these factors create a holistic value proposition that will meet rising consumer expectations.

Competing for the new consumer

| Willingness to pay | RISING CONSUMER EXPECTATIONS | Desire to engage |

- Dynamic offering portfolio
- Individualization
- Convenience
- Holistic solutions
- Unexpected benefits
- New standards of quality

- Active involvement
- Individual recognition and reward
- Increase influence and voice
- Image and identity
- Trust and legitimacy

Enhancing willingness to pay means directly addressing the challenges of commoditization and the dramatic growth in "good enough" products. It means recognizing that, while consumers may not be willing to pay a premium for standard offerings, they will do so for innovative or customizable products of much higher quality. Expanding the benefits and alternatives available to the consumer enhances their consumption experience, and thus willingness to pay, by focusing on needs and wants, not just on price.

But winning the competition is about more than needs, wants, features, and price. The consumer must have a desire to engage with a company and its offerings. While willingness to pay means that businesses can get value from individual transactions, the desire to engage demonstrates the potential for a much deeper, longer-term relationship. Both elements are essential to rethinking the playing field from the consumer perspective.

. . . .

Perspectives from the front line: connected consumers

Daniel Borel Businesses need to understand that customers expect multidimensional products, the co-founder of Logitech told us. *"As we were looking to expand our business, we had a discussion with the executive in charge of TVs at one major supplier. All he was focusing on was cost and cost reduction. These people will lose the battle because all they know is a one-dimensional thing. They don't even see the opportunities out there. All they see is it is a hardware thing, or a software thing."*

Rather than focusing on hardware or software, Borel is responding to the growing consumer demand to manage the interface between people and technology. *"Looking at the world today there are two elements shaping the future: the technology element, which is evolving very fast, and the human factor, [which is] slowing down the rate of change. The issue for businesses like ours is how to bridge the gap between these two and enable progress to accelerate.*

"Essentially we live in the world of the interface. How can we connect people to their technology and enable them to get the most out of it, be it mice or keyboards for computers or remote controls connecting people to their music collections stored in the clouds. This is quite different from looking at the cost of making a simple commodity product."

Sunil Bharti Mittal The founder, chairman and Group CEO of Bharti Enterprises Ltd, explained how telecommunication companies need to rethink their role in future – beyond the pipes. *"Looking ahead, I do not think we will be a telecommunications company, we'll become a lifestyle company. Our industry is changing. People are making fewer calls, they are having more internet sessions and doing more transacting over internet. These are changes we need to adapt to.*

"Today the company has the mindset of a telecom company. But we need to build on our telecom infrastructure to become an internet company. Our mindset has to become more of an internet company, which needs to move fast and which needs to think out of the box. Traditional thinking in telecom companies is very different.

"One important element of this is that our leadership needs to start getting younger, with a mindset to build this future, not continue to focus on building the pipes that has been our challenge in the past. We need younger people to be more innovative, we need them to be more agile. Our industry is going to belong to young people."

Murphy Morobe The former CEO of Kagiso Media in South Africa knows that the best forms of communication allow both sides to make their voice heard. In his company's case, this means that listeners can choose what songs a radio station plays. *"The indigenization of content is very important, because being local can give you global benefits as well,"* he said. *"Consumers want responsiveness and relevance.*

"Take our Jacaranda FM 94.2, radio station, which has a very significant Afrikaans listenership. We've served them for a long time and understand their music and information needs. So we have now created a new entity called JA FM, short for Jacaranda Afrikaans, which is on the internet. It's listener-driven radio, where the audience chooses what it wants to hear next by voting for that song. The song with the most votes gets played first, followed by the next highest and so on. On our FM transmission, our Top 40 chart shows are voted on by audiences and they also select the songs we play through regular research which filters our music library down to only the songs that they want to hear. Audiences shaping their media has never been as easy as it is today with so many social media platforms enhancing the conversation between the radio presenter and her audience. Every show is now a dialog.

"We live in exciting times as media owners who understand that the relationship with our audiences is fundamental to our success. To get that right requires an engagement. It's a very exciting concept, because it speaks to listeners, a group which is in search of affinity and [the feeling that] they have their culture and their interests looked after."

• •

Ask yourself: how will you rethink your playing field as the power of connected consumers continues to rise?

Business will not be at the center of the playing field of the future – the connected consumer or customer will, and they will define what value is, potentially a shifting concept. To succeed in this future, you will need to shape and influence your business's extended networks and the exploding number of channels to the consumer to build reputation, trust, loyalty, returns, market position, and ultimately the license to compete.

Ask yourself:

Markets What do the changes in consumer power and behavior mean for your markets today and in the future?

Value What will be the most important future sources of value for consumers? What will consumers be willing to pay a premium for? How will you position yourself to serve their future needs and wants?

Consumer-controlled communities What does self-segmentation of consumers mean for your markets? How will you identify the most important emerging groups?

Co-creation How can you develop closer relationships with consumers to allow co-creation of products, services, experiences, and value?

Interdependence How will your organization be affected by increasing interdependence with consumers? How will you equip your leaders to understand and work effectively in this environment?

• •

The new war for talent

Consumers care. Consumers want companies to care, and they are prepared to use their power to encourage this.

Consumers are also employees. Companies need to keep this, and the other changing characteristics defining the future consumer, in mind when they think about the new talent landscape.

Increasingly, talented employees want more than a paycheck and the chance to do what they're told to the best of their abilities. Instead, they want jobs that are both exciting and meaningful. They want to work for organizations that care about more than money. They want to work for organizations that are preparing to shape the future – and which encourage employees to find ways to shape the organization itself to do this.

It is not just people's choices that will affect the war for talent, either. Rapid changes in technology, shifting demographic and economic patterns, and speedy diffusion of knowledge worldwide will all play a part. Other factors include smart machines, the rise of the "global brain", and increasingly mobile workforces.

How technology will shape the future of work

Robots and computers already undertake many menial jobs once done by humans, but as they get smarter the types of work they can do will increase; they could end up taking on any repetitive task that can be broken into a series of steps.

Economists have argued that this will reduce the need for mid-level workers, whose jobs can be offshored or ceded to smart machines.[6] The Industrial Revolution principles of division of labor will, in future, be applied to knowledge work. The latest software and hardware already allows amateurs to do what professionals once did, from completing tax returns and trading equities to diagnosing medical conditions.

Online and mobile technologies are making the practicalities of crowdsourcing and open innovation, as described earlier, ever-simpler to manage. This is fortunate, given that companies cannot access all the talent embedded in the "global brain" simply by employing it. Instead, they have to find new ways to find, create, and use the knowledge and expertise inherent in these and other networks.

Mobile technology is also changing where people work. They no longer need, or, in many cases, want, to be tied to one physical location. This creates new possibilities, because businesses can use this technology to link people across geographic boundaries. These virtual teams offer individuals flexibility, and the company access to a deeper pool of expertise. In other cases, this technology is being used for outsourcing tasks to contract workers who contribute particular expertise or pieces of work. Either way, managing virtual teams and virtual (temporary) employees demands new skills of team leaders and senior executives.

....

6   "Angst for the Educated", Schumpeter column, *The Economist*, 3 September, 2011.

The impact of changing generations

It was the baby boomers who started businesses thinking about how different generations behaved. They entered a workplace dominated by members of the "traditionalist" generation, who had loyal, patriotic mindsets, preferred top-down decision-making, and trusted institutions. The incoming boomers, by contrast, tended to question authority, and wanted to put their own stamp on institutions.

Then there was the shift towards members of Generation X, who are more skeptical of institutions, and more self-reliant than their predecessors.

Now the focus is on Generation Y, members of which are typically described as globally concerned, cyberliterate, and media savvy. This group seeks out meaningful work, prefers a partnering style of leadership, and takes a collaborative approach to communication.

Soon they will be followed by the most digitally integrated generation ever: Generation Z. Members of this generation have never known a world in which they could not be in conversation with anyone, anywhere, anytime. For them, boundaries between physical and virtual worlds simply do not exist. But it's not just technology that has shaped them: they have grown up in an era of globalization, global terrorism, and the worst financial crisis since the 1930s.

Employers can secure the commitment of workers from these younger generations by offering them exciting options that allow them to solve issues in ways that stretch their abilities without pigeonholing them. Young workers have an intuitive understanding of the boundaryless nature of the world to come, and have no desire to be placed in a box by someone else. Instead, they expect employers to adapt to their way of thinking, which has been described by some as a playlist approach because of their habit of customizing everything they do from a menu of options.

Companies are also taking into account younger generations' desire to do something that changes the world. They expect work to provide purpose and meaning, not just a salary and career progression – something that may cause particular issues in financial services and other sectors that have traditionally used money to motivate.

But it's not just younger generations that matter. Longer working lives mean that organizations will soon find that their workforce includes people from most, or even all, of these generations. They will need to rethink their talent strategies to attract and motivate each of them. Generational differences need to be taken into account in other ways, too, so that leaders can manage both the potent mix for misunderstandings and conflict, and the huge opportunity for learning between generations.

None of this will be easy; evidence gathered to date suggests that bridging generational gaps is difficult, and that differences between generations are bigger than those between people from the same generation but different countries.

Shifting generations

Born	Traits	Desires	Styles
Traditionalists			
1900-1945	Patriotic, loyal, conservative, have faith in institutions	Help in, or easing into, retirement	Command and control leadership, top down communication, uncomfortable with technology, feel that it's unwise to change jobs
Baby boomers			
1946-1964	Competitive, question authority, desire to put own stamp on institutions, optimistic	Robust careers, help juggling it all	"Get it done" approach to leadership, protective in communication, unsure of technology, feel that changing jobs can be a setback
Generation X			
1965-1980	Eclectic, resourceful, self-reliant, skeptical of institutions, adaptive, independent	Balance and freedom	Want coaching style leadership, network approach to communication, technology is essential for work, changing jobs is necessary
Generation Y (aka millennials, net generation, digital natives, Generation Next, trophy kids)			
1981-1994	Globally concerned, integrated, cyberliterate, media savvy, realistic, environmentally conscious	Meaningful work	Want partnership leadership, collaborative approach to communication, latest technology must be provided, job changing normal and frequent

Born	Traits	Desires	Styles
Generation Z (aka Gen C, iGeneration, net generation, internet generation, digital natives)			
1995-onwards	Globally focused, multicultural, technology in their DNA, always connected, socially and environmentally active, compulsive multitaskers, live in a customized world, short attention spans, ownership less important than experience	Work that constantly stimulates and engages	Desire to customize their own approach versus rigid instructions, expect flexible working and real-time communications, peer-driven, collaborative approach to leadership, networked inside and outside organization, entrepreneurial, always in search of something new

Sources: Strategy Dynamics Global SA analysis from various sources including: BridgeWorks, Lynne Lancaster and David Stillman, authors of When Generations Collide, HarperCollins, 2003; McKinsey Quarterly, Kelly Services, Oxygenz, Pew Research, and Prosumer Report.

Note: In the latter generations, there is still some overlapping terminology as there is no single accepted source for defining generations.

A question of skills: unemployment and unemployability

The global financial crisis did not end the war for talent. If anything, it is about to enter a whole new level.

The World Bank predicts that we need to create 600 million new jobs worldwide in the next 15 years, with a particular emphasis on Asia and sub-Saharan Africa, to keep up with the massive need. That could sound like there are more people seeking work than organizations wanting to employ them, but the labor market is a world of contradictions. Companies are desperate for skilled, talented workers to fill empty positions – yet unemployment rates are skyrocketing. Just what's going on?

It's nothing as simple as poor education, at least in the traditional sense, as each new generation is entering the workforce better qualified than the one before it. In 2010, people aged 15 and over had an average 7.8 years of schooling, up from 3.2 in 1950 and 5.3 in 1980. Between 1950 and 2010 the average number of years of education rose from 6.2 to 11.0 years in high-income countries, and from 2.1 to 7.1 years in low-income countries.

The problem, business leaders told us, is an emerging split between unemployable workers – those who do not have the specific knowledge or skills needed in the future – and the in-demand workers, who have these things in abundance. "Skill development is amongst the single biggest issues that will impact India's growth in the future," Sanjeev Asthana, Founder & Managing Partner of I-Farm Venture Advisors Private Ltd in India, told us. "We have almost 14 million youths coming into the job market every year, and they are largely unskilled. While they can find some form of employment at the most basic level, the difference between them earning US$100 a month and US$300 a month is simple skill sets.

"It's a huge disconnect that in a country like India with a huge pool of labor, the big issue for any industry or services sector is that they don't have enough employable people to work, whether it is in agriculture, textiles, hotels, transport, logistics, you name it. There's a mass of people and a mass of jobs out there but the two are simply not getting matched. There's a difference between unemployment and unemployability. Yes, you're available for employment, but you're not employable because you don't possess the skills required."

This mismatch is not just an issue for India or other B&B countries, but one that is confronting societies and businesses around the world. The only way to reduce it is to make sure that workers are prepared to fill the jobs of the future, which means that governments, educators, and businesses need to rethink education, including who delivers it.

• •

Perspectives from the front line: generations

Shelly Lazarus *"The remarkable thing is how Gen Y approaches balance,"* the chairman emeritus of Ogilvy & Mather told us. *"The generation before the boomers lived to work, the boomers worked to live, and Gen Y just lives.*

"It's as if their work is episodic. Who can now posit an entire talent strategy on the assumption that people will come out of university, join the company, and stay for 45 years? You can't, not now that you have Gen Y who are always thinking about the next thing, and whose average tenure is 16 months.

"What you have to do is figure out whatever it is that they're seeking with a move every 16 months. Can you provide those episodes within the organization? Can you move them fast enough, with enough difference

in the challenge of the assignment, to make it the same thing as changing companies? We have to move young people fast so that they're always challenged, they're always learning – and they don't have time to start to talk to other people about other jobs."

She also told us: "They [members of younger generations] tend to move in tribes. One person moves somewhere else, and then they pluck out the two or three people who were working with them at the last place or two places before, and they regroup at another organization. They kind of recreate their environment themselves – the institution is almost irrelevant.

"The positive part of it is they're pretty engaged. They're less worried about 'where is this company going in the long term,' because they're assumption is that they're not going to be there. But they are interested in the brand in terms of what it stands for. They want to be engaged in something that makes a difference. They want to change the world."

Feike Sijbesma Generation Y employees grew up assuming that team working, collaboration, and (virtual) social connections are a normal part of life. This attitude contains the potential to change organizational structures as well as work habits, the chairman and CEO of DSM, a life sciences company, told us.

"They have completely different ways of using information and working, and I see that as a challenge, perhaps not in five to 10 years but maybe in 10 to 15 years," he said. "We will need to organize ourselves differently into a much more networked style of organization, which is different than the way we are structured now with one guy on the top.

"While we would not do that today, because the organization works well, we can't postpone the change for 10 years. We are already experimenting around this today, but I think in 10 to 15 years, we're going to have to address the real issue, because then those guys are not 15 years old anymore. They will be 30 and getting into more senior positions here.

"This change to a next generation which is much more used to working in flat networks, provides many opportunities to deal better with the increasingly fast, complex and global nature of businesses."

Patrik Andersson "To attract these people, you need to think about the whole package around the workplace and the work itself," the former CEO of Rieber & Son, the food company, told us. "We need to think about work-life balance, because they don't want to work as much we have done, and *they want to develop themselves. I don't think the career as such is that important, or the need they have for decent money. They don't go to work just to work. It's more than that. It's about sharing and belonging.*

"Corporate social responsibility and the values of the company are going to become much more important. The younger generations want to know what your company stands for, what it does, and how it behaves. That's going to be crucial in attracting them."

• •

Ask yourself: does your company have the talent it needs?

It's all well and good rethinking your playing field in terms of markets, competitors, and consumers, but without the right people your organization will not be able to deliver. Rethinking the war on talent is about harnessing new technologies and the shifting pool of people available in order to realize your place in the new playing field.

Ask yourself:

Adding value How will the workplace, and the talent pool, of the future affect your company's ability to create both value and new business models? How will it help you to deliver on them?

Knowhow What technologies and capabilities will your organization's talent need to harness or build so that it can deliver to its customers?

Development What can or should your business be doing to develop these technologies and capabilities? How far can you expect government, educators, and other stakeholders to do it?

Attract and motivate Do you need to rethink what you do and how you do it, so that you can attract and motivate the brightest talent?

Balance How will you balance business continuity and success with the episodic nature of work in future?

• •

Society's expectations are changing

Business leaders who believe that their sole responsibility is making money for shareholders don't feel the need to worry much about their company's relationship to society at large. They can't get caught breaking laws or regulations, obviously, because fines or criminal proceedings would not look good on the books, but that is as far as they feel that they need to go.

We argue that this approach has always been morally and ethically wrong, but it is fast becoming a very bad idea strategically, too. Society's expectations of business are clearly changing. It is no longer enough for companies to avoid breaking the rules, nor to have a few, isolated corporate social responsibility (CSR) activities; they need to take an active approach to improving the world around them or risk losing the trust of customers, employees, institutions, and communities.

Companies that have lost the public trust have always struggled with the fallout that a damaged reputation causes their business, but the impact will be worse in years to come. The networked, connected nature of the future means, as we discussed earlier, that companies will be more dependent than ever before on their relationships with all stakeholders – relationships that will suffer if trust falls – and that critics can make their voices heard around the world within an incredibly short space of time.

As an example of the rising importance of societal issues for business, one CEO told us "Whatever business you are in, if you are not taking care about the environment and sustainability and the economy, it's like a CEO of a company saying 'I can continue to grow without the internet' in 1995."

The business-society ladder

Many companies have started rethinking their playing field in the light of changing social expectations, with business leaders describing a wide range of approaches, as set out in the business-society ladder.

The business-society ladder

	Focus of societal activities	Responsible unit	Output/impact on the business
Level 1:	Philanthropy or propaganda; meeting legal requirements	CSR as a separate function	Charitable activities and/or "greenwashing" promotions; compliance with regulations
Level 2:	Focused partnerships in areas of significant mutual benefit	CSR as a separate function, with authority in specific areas	Strengthens firm operations; delivers mutual benefits to society and firm within targeted areas
Level 3:	Shaping strategy, business models and activities to ensure "permissibility"	Core element of top management agenda; CSR integrated into operations and strategies	Reshapes how the business operates; earns the license to operate and grow in the future
Level 4:	Shaping the objectives and direction of the company; aligning the company's core purpose with societal needs	Core element of top management agenda; CSR integrated into operations, strategy, purpose, and direction	Fundamentally reshapes why, how, and where the business operates; delivers shared value/ prosperity; impacts all decision-making

Even before we start describing the levels in the ladder above, it is worth noting that there are firms which conform to regulations governing their industry but have little further interest in social responsibility. The only exception to this comes when a chairman or CEO uses his or her role to support pet projects or individual causes.

The leader of one such company told us: "If a person thinks that sustainability is more important than profit, they should quit and work for an NGO. We are not an NGO, we are a company and the best thing that we can do for society is to generate sustainable wealth." This sums up the prevailing attitude in such firms rather nicely.

Level one Companies in this category as well as meeting legal requirements often make a lot of noise about their CSR activities, but these deliver only marginal benefits to either society or the business. Most have established a CSR function but have not given it the power to make any changes to the firm's core activities or operations. They may be involved in corporate philanthropy, although this is likely to be limited to financial donations. CSR activities are usually designed to maximize marketing and public relations opportunities, rather than with a focus on their underlying substance; the results can look like propaganda or "green washing."

Level two Organizations at this level have a true social responsibility agenda, typically involving active partnering with other stakeholders in areas of significant mutual interest, as well as a philosophy of taking responsibility for its impact on society. These partnerships, which tend to be built around a sustainable agenda, deliver significant benefits to all involved. CSR activities are usually supported or driven by a separate function, as at level one, but at this level the function has real authority and the ability to shape the firm's activities, albeit only in certain specified areas.

There are many examples of level two partnerships at Unilever (tea), Nestlé (coffee), Mars (cocoa), and other companies which purchase significant quantities of farming raw materials. While the firms require sustainable supplies of raw materials to support their businesses, the supplying farms and communities can benefit from investment in improving productivity and sustainability. These partnerships provide a natural linkage to meet the interests of the businesses and society.

For example, Mars, a major global food manufacturer with a strong commitment to social responsibility, depends on a sustainable supply of high-quality cocoa. With demand for cocoa rising, supply is not expected to keep pace given that it is sourced through labor-intensive processes, mostly in developing countries. Farmers there struggle with aging trees, pests and disease, depleted soil, and poor access to training and other resources. In response, Mars has launched a cocoa sustainability program to help farmers produce better crops and make more money for their families. The ultimate goal of this initiative is to create a sustainable supply of quality cocoa, with farmers being empowered to reinvest in their businesses and communities.

Level three At this level, leaders have a clear vision of what it will take for their business to be successful in the future, and are shaping and reshaping their company accordingly. This vision incorporates a strong understanding of the relationship between business and society. At this level, senior management, not a specialized function, has responsibility for the business's overall relationship with society, which means that it is integrated into strategy development and can shape the business's agenda. The result is that the firm's direct and indirect impacts on society become integral to organizational activity. Often leaders of such companies will talk about these activities in terms of developing permissible business models and earning the license to operate and grow in the future.

Unilever is a good example of level three. The company has made a commitment to halve environmental impact at the same time it doubles its business. A key element of this effort is their Sustainable Living Plan, described below.

Level four Shared value, also known as linked prosperity or a host of other names, shapes the agenda of companies operating at this level. This approach, recently highlighted and popularized by Michael Porter in a Harvard Business Review article, involves rethinking and altering not just what the firm does, but its fundamental purpose, the value it creates, and how this value is shared.

We met many firms whose leaders told us they intended to take this approach, but our experience suggests that many leaders and firms talk about being at levels three and four, while their activities seem more closely associated with levels one and two. Many companies talked about creating shared value scorecards, for example, but these were often applied only after they were sure that they had met the traditional financial and performance scorecard.

We encountered two firms that were clearly operating at level four: Ben & Jerry's, the U.S. ice-cream company now owned by Unilever, and Mahindra Group, a multinational business based in India. They place their relationship with society at the center of their strategies, using it to shape not only how they operate, but also what activities and businesses they undertake. We share their stories in more detail in the next chapter.

For more detail on how companies are rethinking their relationship with society, see "Making the Most of Corporate Social Responsibility," by Tracey Keys, Thomas Malnight and Kees van der Graaf, which was published in the December 2009 issue of McKinsey Quarterly. To read more about shared value, see "Creating Shared Value", by Michael E. Porter and Mark R. Kramer, which was published in the January 2011 issue of Harvard Business Review.

Unilever's Sustainable Living Plan

Unilever wants to double the size of its business while reducing its overall environmental impact. Its Sustainable Living Plan is designed to deliver three key outcomes by 2020:

1. Help more than a billion people take action to improve their health and wellbeing.

2. Decouple the company's growth from its environmental impact across the product lifecycle, with the goal of halving the environmental footprint of the making and use of Unilever products.

3. Enhance the livelihoods of hundreds of thousands of people in the company's supply chain.

These goals are supported by targets and associated metrics in seven core areas.

Health and hygiene Help more than a billion people improve their hygiene habits; bring safe drinking water to 500 million people to help reduce the incidence of life-threatening diseases such as diarrhea.

Nutrition Double the proportion of the company's portfolio that meets the highest nutritional standards to help people achieve a healthier diet.

Greenhouse gases Halve the greenhouse gas impact of the firm's products across their lifecycles.

Water Halve the water associated with consumer use of Unilever products.

Waste Halve the waste associated with disposal of the firm's products.

Sustainable sourcing All palm oil to be sourced sustainably by 2015, and all agricultural raw materials by 2020.

Better livelihoods Link more than 500,000 smallholder farmers and small-scale distributors into the company's supply chain.

What makes this plan different

Five elements of this plan make it stand out from other sustainability initiatives.

First, the company has put sustainability at the heart of its vision, strategy, and brand portfolio. This is not a CSR department dreaming up some great, isolated initiatives which run independently of day-to-day business, but an integral part of the company's operations. The company will be held to account on whether or not it hits the targets it has shared publicly as part of the plan.

Second, the plan mobilizes and engages the entire organization. Everyone in the company has a role and, more importantly, clear, inspiring, and energizing ambitions towards which they can aim. This creates the potential for unprecedented employee engagement.

Third is the way in which the company has focused its energies outward, not inward. The plan incorporates a complete lifecycle analysis of the company's products and their impact, enabling Unilever to understand where its efforts can make most difference – sourcing raw materials and changing how consumers use their products.

Next, the plan breaks big problems into small steps, making it easier for consumers, employees, and suppliers to see how they can get involved and make a difference. Finally, and connected with the fourth point, the plan recognizes that Unilever can't do it alone, and emphasizes the importance of partnering with governments, NGOs, suppliers, and others.

So, that's the plan. Is it working? Unilever's 2012 results, announced in January 2013, suggest that it is. Revenue rose 10.5% and net profit grew by 7% despite very difficult conditions in developed markets. The company's sustainability progress report for 2011 showed double-digit growth in brands such as Lifebuoy and Comfort, which are building sustainability into their offers; good levels of savings from packaging reduction and eco-efficiency programs in factories; and 24% of agricultural materials sustainably sourced, up from 14% in 2010. The report also showed that it was doing less well than it hoped in some areas, including carbon emissions.

• •

Perspectives from the front line: society

Paul Polman *"The importance of the role of business in society has always been there, but I think the [financial] crisis has made it come alive even more,"* the CEO of Unilever told us. *"The real issue is how to get permission to be successful.*

"It's very clear that the parameters here are rapidly changing. I believe that it is essential for any business that is going to grow and be successful over the long term to always think carefully about how to get permission from society to grow and be successful."

Paul Michaels Mars, the family-owned food company, is committed to a triple bottom line (people, profit, planet), but also wants to broaden and deepen its relationships with consumers, its CEO told us. *"The ultimate competitive advantage for any company comes from selling products that have higher order benefits with consumers,"* he said. *"Our goal is that every major brand aligns with a social responsibility plank that makes sense for them. We're not there yet, but this is clearly our intention."*

Shelly Lazarus *"The market has spoken,"* the chairman emeritus of Ogilvy & Mather told us. *"The market cares. People care. They want you to be socially responsible or they will dismiss you as a legitimate company."*

Feike Sijbesma *"If you look at success as a pure economist, then you may well conclude that profit is the highest value,"* the chairman and CEO of Royal DSM told us. *"From a purely economic point of view, that might be true. But companies are also a part of society, and you cannot measure the success of one without reference to the success of the others. We need to learn that we have to create value on three dimensions simultaneously, all balanced equally: societal, environmental and economic. I call that People, Planet and Profit".*

Sijbesma and his team are using insights about societal change – particularly climate change, the global imbalance of food and health, and the effects of globalization – to guide the company's transformation. His goal is to find ways that DSM can solve some of the challenges that these changes pose.

"We focus on life sciences and materials sciences," Sijbesma said. *"That's about improving health and food where we can, but it's also about things like making cars lighter, which helps with the energy and climate change problem."*

• •

Ask yourself: how must you think your business's relationship with society?

Gabriela Alvarez, a colleague who has researched this area extensively, has a simple way of describing many companies' efforts to rethink their relationship with society: visionaries at the top, missionaries at the bottom, and managers stuck in between. That is, many firms have committed idealists at the top and bottom of the hierarchy, but so many bureaucratic processes, systems, and ways of working in the middle that nothing actually changes. Keep this in mind when considering how society is changing the playing field – and how you are changing your organization in response.

Ask yourself:

Mutual benefit How do you help to meet the needs and demands of consumers and other stakeholders with respect to socially important issues? Does this allow for mutual benefits?

The ladder Where are you on the Business-Society Ladder? Where do you want to be?

Relationships What capabilities will you need to build so that your relationship with society is one of mutual benefit and shared value? What other aspects of your organization and its agenda will you need to rethink?

Stakeholders Which external stakeholders will you need to work with for future success? How will you work with them?

• •

Rethink your playing field: recap

Your competitors are not who you think they are Competition is no longer the preserve of other firms that look, act, and think like you do. The future is being shaped by cross-industry competition with firms that provide different offerings and value propositions that focus on the same consumer and customer needs, wants, and demands that your firm does.

Growth markets are changing Many developed market firms see geographic expansion as the answer to short-term growth pressures, but the fight to own the high-growth markets of the future reflects further, deeper challenges. Competition in and for growth markets is not just happening between businesses, but also between mindsets, as players with different resources, business models, home market systems, and outlooks compete for the markets of the future.

Consumers are changing Businesses often talk about the fight to own the consumer – that is, to control the relationships and shape consumers' buying choices – but it is consumers themselves who are winning the fight. Consumers across geographies, and generations, are gaining power, influence, and choice. They are demanding more from businesses, and are less willing to pay for it.

The new war for talent There is a growing difference between the unemployed, the unemployable, and the in-demand future talent. There are also changes in what employees expect of the companies for which they work, particularly as younger generations enter the workforce. They expect companies to adapt to them, not the other way around.

Society's expectations, and demands, are changing Social expectations of business used to revolve around regulatory and legal compliance, but this is changing; business is now expected to make a positive contribution to society in return for a license to operate. These expectations are leading many companies to rethink their relationship with society not just as an add-on to business activities, but as a core element that shapes their strategies and activities for the future.

Let's return briefly to two-directional thinking, the idea we introduced in chapter two when we talked about bridging the gap between short-term and long-term success. While many of the changes we talk about in this chapter might seem long-term in nature – because they are – the shifts are already happening, and businesses will need to start work today to build the capabilities, business models and mindsets to win in the new reality of tomorrow.

Putting two-directional thinking into action when rethinking your playing field means starting with the future. It means actively throwing away the boxes that have characterized your organization's past environment. Instead, identify what your future environment will look like from the perspective of competition, markets, consumers, talent, and societal expectations. What must you do to achieve the position you want in this future? What do you have to start doing now to be ready for the future – and to shape your place in it? Next, switch lenses and look at today's picture. Consider the possible paths and options that would allow you to move from today to the future you have defined. What are the gaps you need to address?

Rethinking your playing field requires you as a leader and your organization to take on five key challenges:

1. Build your understanding of how long-term global trends are affecting your business, markets, competitors, and consumers.

2. Find out how the people and institutions who can influence the world are changing, and understand how these changes will impact and shape your future.

3. Understand how society's expectations of business are changing, and what this means for your company and your leaders.

4. Look at your playing field through multiple lenses – consumer, NGO, baby boomer, digital native, and so on – to avoid letting old assumptions bias your perspective. Remember: throw away the boxes.

5. Use insights gained through two-directional thinking to challenge your current business models, activities, and mindsets so that you can identify threats and opportunities.

Measure your progress

Use this table to assess whether you and your organization are rethinking your playing field effectively. As before, key ideas introduced in this chapter are set out in the shaded rows of text. The numbered columns describe the different characteristics of progress for each, with 1 describing the least advanced and 5 describing the most advanced state of practice in companies today. Options 2 or 4 mean your company is somewhere in between each state of practice.

Again, we suggest leaders go through this assessment twice: once answering from their organization's perspective, and once from their own personal position. Have others in your senior leadership team – as well as people lower down the organization and even your broader stakeholders – complete the exercise independently to gain additional insights.

1	2	3	4	5
View of competition				
Our competitors provide the same products and services as we do		We innovate within our existing market boundaries to stay ahead of competition		We shape future markets, and our business, in collaboration with stakeholders

1	2	3	4	5
Relationship with shapers & influencers				
We control our own destiny		We have partnerships in selected areas of immediate concern		We collaborate with multiple stakeholders to co-create our future markets and business
Approach to growth markets				
We approach all markets in the same way, using our traditional portfolio of products and services and business model		We adapt our portfolio, business model and approach to take account of local differences		We design and develop our portfolio, business models and approaches to provide value in different markets and economic systems
View of customers/consumers				
Our existing products and services meet customers' needs; we know what customers/consumers want		We lead innovation in our current markets based on current customer/consumer needs, delivering value through experiences		We constantly redefine our business and offerings around customer/consumer needs based on meaningful relationships to co-create experiences and value
Approach to talent				
Our recruitment processes are adequate to source the people and skills we need		We focus on retention, motivation, and involving our employees, and are developing new approaches for younger generations		The power of our talent is released by empowering them and engaging them behind the direction and purpose of the company
Relationship with society				
We exist to make a profit for our owners; our relationship with society is based on compliance with regulations and limited philanthropic activities		We have focused partnerships with key stakeholders to achieve mutual benefits; our relationship with society is based on permissible business models		Our relationship with society is based on the concept of shared value/prosperity
Two-directional thinking				
We plan and budget for incremental improvements on today's performance; we minimize risks in all our decision making		We have a general idea of where we want to be in future and what that will require us to do, but planning is generally from today forwards		We actively think from both directions, challenging our current business models, activities, and mindsets; we manage a portfolio of business and market options

85

THREE: Redefine Your Ambition

Initiatives are easy.

See a problem, launch an initiative. See an opportunity, launch an initiative.

They are also exhausting, and, worse, they can create a false sense of security. After all, this much activity must mean that challenges are being addressed and preparations for the future are being made, right?

Don't be so sure. Busyness does not mean that an organization is moving in the right direction. It may mean that it is not moving at all: initiatives developed to meet short-term goals are likely to keep companies in the short-term trap. Actions need to be built around a clearly defined ambition, which should itself be founded on a point of view on the future, and what it will take to succeed there.

In the last chapter we looked at how and why leaders need to rethink their playing field. Redefining your ambition, the second of the 3Rs, works hand-in-hand with this concept. This stage is about leaders taking their new understanding of the changes ahead and using it to explore alternatives, and make choices, about the direction in which their organization must move to be successful in the future.

Those who do not redefine their ambition in light of the changes to come will find it difficult, if not impossible, to bridge the gap between short and long-term demands. Leaders have to know where they want their organization to go if they hope to do more than hold on to the past. This includes taking proactive actions, as opposed to reactive responses to immediate pressures.

While this book is not about capitalism as such, the issues we raise in this chapter – and which Paul Polman raises in his foreword about responsible capitalism – are a critical part of the picture. Businesses redefining their own ambitions and playing a more proactive role in society will have a clear impact on the economic and social systems that evolve in the future.

Do you know where you are going, and why?

When we ask executives how they use their company's purpose and vision to make day-to-day decisions the usual answer is blunt: they don't. This response is often accompanied by a strange look, as if asking such a question demonstrates that we have a fundamental misunderstanding of business. Such things, the look seems to suggest, are relevant only to marketing departments, and need not be the concern of any other leader.

Stop for a second and think about the implications of this attitude. It means that executives are not leading their businesses, in any meaningful sense; after all, how can someone lead without a vision of the path ahead? Our research indicates that such an attitude is nearly always a marker of an organization that does not know where it is going to be in the future, let alone why it is going to be there. Very few such companies have started bridging the gap; instead, they are focused almost entirely on protecting the present, or even the past.

Organizations that want to prepare for the future need to redefine their ambition. That is, they need to redefine what they do and why they do it. In this chapter, we address three fundamental questions that leaders must ask themselves during the redefinition process: Why does my company exist? What do I want my company to look like in the future? And how can I ensure that I am making the changes today needed for success tomorrow? Or, to put it another way, what is my purpose, what is my vision, and what metrics will I use to measure success?

Redefining your ambition

These three questions seem simple enough, but many organizations struggle to keep the concepts separate, which prevents them from developing the clarity they need in their answers. The executive comfort zone, which we talked about in Bridging the Gap, adds to the difficulty, because many people are uncomfortable with any discussion that may require them to change.

Why are we asking you to redefine each of these areas, rather than simply defining them? It's part of bridging the gap: most established companies already have at least some of the underlying foundations in place, so redefining rather than starting from scratch keeps that connection between winning in the present and preparing to win in the future.

That said, leaders need to keep an open mind throughout the process, as there may be areas in which their redefinition needs to be so fundamental that it is effectively a definition from scratch. That is what it will take if a bank is to compete with a mobile phone company – and vice versa.

Such changes cannot be made in a year, or brought about through an acquisition. They take time, effort, and visionary leadership. They require executives to get to the core of what their company does and does not do – and why. They need people to make choices.

And, ultimately, these choices need a leader to have a sense of destination, if not of destiny. They need a point of view on what will happen in the world outside their organization – that's why they have to rethink their playing fields – but they also need to know where the organization itself should move. That's where the second of the 3Rs comes in.

● ●

Perspectives from the front line: ambition

Kan Trakulhoon *"We used to say that we wanted to be the role model in all our key areas of activity,"* the president and CEO of SCG, the Thai conglomerate, told us. *"But now we are going beyond this and striving for even more. If you are just a role model, it means you do something well or better than others, and then you wait for others to follow you. But for us looking forward, we must move outside our current territory and activities. After we enter and excel in these new areas, we will then be able to think about how to bring others to follow us."*

Fabio Schvartsman *"Klabin is a very traditional company, more than 114 years old,"* the paper company's CEO told us. *"Many companies in Brazil are much younger. This company went from generation to generation in the same family. It used to be one of the biggest companies in the country, but it lost ground during the last 20 years, and now is making a steady recovery. I'll be very happy if we can bring back Klabin to the same kind of importance in Brazil that it had in the past.*

"We will measure this success by what the company is doing, how it is innovating, what it is creating for our people, for our environment and society, and for the shareholders, and how it is transforming itself to be able to be a true leading multinational. Our success will create a company that will be a symbol for the future, and a company that will help transform the country into a much more modern and much more global country than it is today."

William Heinecke *"If you asked me what I think is our greatest achievement, it is that we provide employment for many, many people,"* the chairman and CEO of Minor International Plc., the Thai hospitality company, told us. *"We're a major user of local products. We touch many hundreds of thousands of people because of what we buy – all fresh local produce. So we're having a direct impact on this economy and we must always continue to do that. This is something that is worthwhile.*

"To me, if we employ 200,000 people five years from now, and if we touch many more thousands of lives, expanding also into other parts of the world, I would believe that we have achieved something more than just a monetary success factor."

- -

Looking beyond today: Stora Enso Pathfinders

Jouko Karvinen, the CEO of Stora Enso of Finland, led a dramatic financial turnaround at the paper and packaging company. However, he recognized that the company still faced important long-term challenges. "While we have financially turned around the business, we have not solved the fundamental challenges we face," he said. "We have only bought ourselves a few more years to figure out where we want to take this business."

His response was the Pathfinder Program. Working with IMD, Karvinen chose 12 people from across his organization and told them: "You're fired. Go out in to the world and find out what others, the true best-in-class, are doing. Then come back and challenge what we are doing and where we are today. Finally use these insights to help us define and shape our future." A key condition was stretching the company's thinking, but not with half-baked dreams; he asked that every idea be paired with a proposal for how the business can start moving there today.

The employees, who were not actually fired, dedicated 30% of their time to this effort. They spent nine months investigating how some of the best companies around the world were tackling innovation and global responsibility before coming to IMD. They visited best-in-class companies in Europe, Brazil, China, India, and other markets. They developed their own frameworks that let them draw out the most interesting thinking from each company and compare it with their own business's practices.

When they began the journey, Stora Enso was a paper and packaging company that was built around the products it manufactured. When they came back, they suggested that the company think about itself differently: as a firm that can develop and build business solutions addressing major societal problems. A key element of their transition was moving from focusing on products in a maturing market to developing capabilities, and businesses, in areas of high growth today and looking to the future.

Purpose matters, or at least it should

Why does your company exist?

The answer, whatever it may be, is its purpose.

Purpose is the fundamental reason why your organization exists. It shapes how other stakeholders see you, what they expect of you, and whether or not they choose to associate with you. Purpose – sometimes referred to as a company's mission – shapes and guides what an organization does and does not do. It gives meaning to those inside the organization.

Despite the impression created by many official mission statements drawn up by marketing departments, a purpose does not have to be positive to have an impact. Let's take two extreme examples to highlight this point.

An investment bank's purpose, for example, might be to make as much money as possible for its staff, shareholders, and clients. This purpose, which the bank might not ever make explicit, will shape everything from its strategy to its hiring preferences, as one of our interviewees, a senior banking executive, made clear.

"Investment banking – although this sounds terribly arrogant – relies on the fact that it gets the best brains," he told us. "Probably per square inch, there is a greater brainpower in this building than you could find in most any other building anywhere. We attract these individuals because we pay them through the nose. And we retain them because we continue to pay them through the nose."

This executive went on to characterize the bank's strategy as "hustle" – that is, work hard and find opportunities. The executive suggested that if new regulations were introduced to limit banks, there were enough smart people in the industry to figure out how to make even more money based on any new regulations.

Reflect on what type of individuals this organization would attract, and what kind of behavior it would promote. Consider what expectations this would create for stakeholders and what decisions it would promote in looking to the future. And then contrast this with the purpose of the Mahindra Group, outlined in more detail later in this chapter. Its mission states: "We will challenge conventional thinking and innovatively use all our resources to drive positive change in the lives of our stakeholders and communities across the world, to enable them to rise." This purpose has not been at the expense of success, as the company's stock price increased more than 20 times between 2002 and 2012, but rather has been a key enabler shaping and directing the dramatic growth and expansion of the company, including deciding what businesses to enter, and not enter, and how to operate in each business.

Again, reflect on what type of individuals this organization would attract, and what kind of behavior it would promote. Consider what expectations this would create for stakeholders and what decisions it would promote in looking to the future.

Our point is not that investment banks are bad and Mahindra Group is good. In and of itself, purpose is a value-free concept. It simply reflects a choice made by a particular company or group of individuals. Theoretically, at least, no one type of purpose is better or worse than another as long as it forms a coherent foundation for the decisions an organization takes. But it does have consequences.

Why a positive purpose matters

In practice, the nature of a company's purpose makes a very big difference precisely because it underpins so many decisions. It matters to shareholders, employees, consumers, and other stakeholders, all of whom will have opinions about what they want in any organization with which they are associated. Some will surely be attracted by the investment banking approach, while others will be drawn to the Mahindra Group approach.

A positive purpose is one which puts something more than money at the heart of an organization's existence. This fundamental decision will go on to shape other decisions in a way that will help leaders to bridge the gap; a positive purpose is almost always aligned with long-term sustainable success rather than short-term profit. There are a number of factors at play here.

One of the most obvious is trust: more specifically, there are low and generally declining levels of trust in institutions, and in business in particular. This is often linked to a perception – maybe even a reality – that companies have a win-at-all-costs mentality that leads them to focus entirely on protecting their own interests, no matter what else is happening in the world. This lack of trust in turn makes it harder to establish and grow effective relationships with stakeholders – something that is becoming increasingly important as the world becomes more interdependent and more connected.

Of course, not all companies have a single-minded focus on securing profit ahead of anything else. Many are trying to do the right thing in a broader sense, even if they are not always successful. Unfortunately for them, this loss of trust is a generalized issue. The problem is that people have lost trust in business, not that some people have lost trust in some businesses. Unless companies have a clear purpose and a reputation for living up to what they believe in, they will not be able to distinguish themselves from the mass of businesses tarnished by mistrust. People will assume that the absence of a clear positive purpose means the presence of a profit-first purpose, even if this was not explicitly stated. This may not be an unreasonable assumption; our research suggests that companies without any clear purpose tended to drift in this direction.

Interestingly, many employees want to work for just such a purpose-driven organization. Many workers, particularly from younger generations, assess job opportunities not just on salary, benefits, and career progression, but on whether their potential employer's purpose and values align with their own. They want to know what impact they can have on the world with their employer, and what positive contribution they can make. Leaders who want to attract and keep the most talented individuals will need to create a purpose-driven organization, and then make sure that every individual within it knows how they can contribute to that purpose. If employees don't believe that they will bring value to the world in a particular role, then they probably won't take it, and if they do take it, they won't stay.

Then there's the hardest reason to quantify: having a positive purpose is simply the right thing to do. Many of the leaders we interviewed saw this as a critical part of their leadership legacy. They did not want to be judged purely on their financial achievement; as Feike Sijbesma put it in the last chapter, companies are part of society, and you cannot measure the success of one without reference to the success of others.

• •

Perspectives from the front line: purpose

Bengt Braun Social considerations form an intrinsic part of how Braun, the former CEO and current vice-chairman of the board at Bonnier, the family-owned media business, thinks about his company's purpose. He expects this purpose to shape how his executives respond to challenges; a quick answer is not always the best.

"A much better way is to define what is right to do and then do it," he tells them. *"Start by thinking about who has an interest in the company: the ownership, the suppliers, the advertisers, the employees, the unions, the board, the management, and whoever else it might be.*

"Then make a wish list for each of these by asking 'what do each of these groups want?' Employees might want more pay, bigger bonuses, better job security, for example.

"Then you pull all those wish lists together and boil it down to what things must be in place for that to have a chance to happen."

Paul Polman Business needs permission from society to be successful, the CEO of Unilever told us, but this brings its own challenges. *"Be aware that some in society will treat business as someone to blame when problems arise,"* he said. *"So when you see the economy like this, you have to blame someone. When people are obese, some blame the food companies, for example.*

"Broadly, the role of business is to earn people's respect. And I think that, despite what you hear from a lot of vocal individuals, respect for companies like ours is fairly high in many places in the world. We have to ensure that we continue to strengthen that respect. Trust has to be earned every day."

Peter Staude Tongaat Hulett is an agricultural company, but its purpose is more than producing and selling food. Governments cannot solve the world's problems alone, so it is business's responsibility, Staude told us, to help create the environment for success.

"We are not only in agriculture and food, but also in land development," the South Africa-based CEO said. *"We sometimes expand on our business description by saying we want to create successful rural communities in the areas where we operate. We want people who live and work in those rural areas to say, 'This is a great place to work, a great place to live, and a great place to bring up kids.' This is the direction we're working towards for all sorts of reasons."*

The company's purpose shapes where Tongaat Hulett operates, what it does – for example, it is moving into long-term partnerships with governments to help develop land and energy resources – and how it operates.

Staude's personal purpose aligns with that of his company. *"I want my organization, my country and my region to perform. I am really passionate about this region and its people. I see all this possibility, I see the many people that really want to improve their lives and their economic reality."*

• •

Purpose and profit go hand in hand: Mahindra Group

It took Anand Mahindra a while to realize the importance of a clear – and clearly expressed – unifying vision of the Mahindra Group's purpose. "In 2002, I thought that we were doing everything right," Mahindra, the Indian multinational's chairman told us.

"We were number one or two in all of our businesses, we were going global, and we were innovators, but our stock price was languishing at about 60 rupees. One board member came to me and warned me that the company was heading for bankruptcy. At the time, I thought he was exaggerating."

When a second person told Mahindra that his stock price should be closer to 500 rupees, he recognized that there was a problem. "We weren't focusing enough on our stakeholders' fears by communicating the fact that what we were doing was leading to good financial outcomes. That was when I began to articulate a core purpose. People needed me to go out on a limb and say: 'This is what we are trying to do. If you understand it, come on board. It's going to be fun.'"

A year later, his stock price hit 250 rupees; by 2012, after adjusting for stock splits, it was about 2,000.

Mahindra does not want to be a saint but he does expect the group's companies to make a positive difference to the world. That means operating on the principle of shared value rather than treating social responsibility as an add-on to be thought about after profit targets have been hit.

"We are not trying to be Mother Teresa," he said. "That's not the point. But companies that don't engage in projects that also create value for society are quickly eroding their brand, and they are losing the trust of the public."

India, with its young, aspirational population and significant levels of poverty, means that a business model based on shared value is a particular opportunity, he said. "The extreme levels of deprivation of a large population of this country are sometimes overlooked because of the euphoria about India rising, but they present an opportunity to have a major positive impact on society.

"But this isn't only an Indian opportunity. Business is facing a huge and growing trust and credibility deficit, which is not good for business or for society. Shared value is something that businesses around the world will have to adopt."

THREE: REDEFINE YOUR AMBITION

Mahindra wants the business to become a purpose-driven organization. He sums up that purpose in one word: Rise. "The Rise manifesto has three pillars: we will accept no limits, we will think alternatively, and we will drive positive change in everything we do," he said. "We will not do anything that doesn't pass the filter of driving real positive change.

"And, if you look at our businesses today, you will see that most of our fastest-growing, most profitable businesses are actually driving the biggest positive change. Everyone is very clear that there are no trade-offs between fulfilling our purpose and creating profitable businesses – we don't separate the two. You have to drill into people's heads that there is no distinction, because you will make more money if you're creating shared value."

Mahindra & Mahindra Limited stock price evolution versus Bombay Stock Exchange, SENSEX (Indexed, 07/01/2002 = 100)

Source: Yahoo! Finance

Ask yourself: have you redefined your purpose?

Knowing why your company exists – not just what products it makes or services it provides – is an essential part of preparing for the future. A positive purpose provides the center that gives stability and continuity while freeing you to make the changes needed to grasp and shape the opportunities of the future. It also unleashes the passion and emotion that will help drive success.

Ask yourself:

Purpose Why does your organization exist? Is that purpose explicit or implicit? How does it shape decisions regarding the future direction of your company? How does your purpose attract and shape relationships with other stakeholders? Ultimately, does it unleash the organization's passion?

Choice Does your purpose allow you to make the choices and decisions needed to be successful in the future? Does it help your employees to define what is right and then do it?

Practicality How can you use purpose to guide everyday decision making across your organization?

• •

A three-part mission: Ben & Jerry's

Can buying a pint of ice cream help to bring about world peace? Ben & Jerry's, the company that puts its social purpose at the heart of how it does business, thinks so. Its mission is based on the idea that creating shared value with partners means that everyone benefits.

When Ben Cohen and Jerry Greenfield founded the company they were determined that it would do more than make high-quality ice cream – although that was part of it, too. When they formalized their values in 1988, the company came up with a three-part mission statement that emphasized product quality, economic reward, and a commitment to the community. "If you take an approach where you are building on our mission-driven linked prosperity, you are lifting people out of poverty and you are creating a more sustainable means of economic wealth in an emerging or developing community," said Rob Michalak, the firm's social mission director.

For example, it uses a bakery in New York that hires, trains and supports homeless people, and pays a premium to dairy farmers so that they don't use bovine growth hormone. When milk prices crashed by 25% in 1991, Cohen announced that the company would pay farmers an above-market rate. The half-million dollars that this cost, he said, would "come out of our profits, where it doesn't belong, and into farmers' pockets, where it does belong." It also ties to how they treat their employees, who are offered everything from profit-share programs to college tuition.

Ben & Jerry's commitment to society, however, goes beyond those with whom it has direct contact.

The company has been an advocate for equal rights since it was founded more than 30 years ago. It was one of the first in the U.S. to expand its health and employment benefits to all unmarried domestic partners, and it is now campaigning for gay and lesbian people to have the same marriage rights as their heterosexual peers. It donates 7.5% of its pre-tax profits to charities.

This sense of social purpose is so important to the company's identity that, when it was acquired by Unilever in 2000, it was set up as a semi-independent business so that it could continue to pursue its three-part mission. It is worth noting that the company's social mission is overseen by an independent board of directors, with only two Unilever representatives out of nine board members. However, the journey has not been straightforward; maintaining its core values while scaling up to become a global business has been challenging.

The firm's leaders also identified challenges and opportunities around what linked prosperity would mean in the future. They described an opportunity to move from an approach centered on maintaining the world's resources and paying a fair price, towards one that would position the business as a positive agent for change. They also talked about how Ben & Jerry's was at a crossroads, and needed to think beyond programs to the re-radicalization of the business and the brand. This was uncharted territory that required the firm to address a number of questions. For example, if sustainability is about maintaining and preserving the world for future generations, should linked prosperity go beyond this to help the world progress? And, if so, what should progress look like? Even for Ben & Jerry's, the challenges of living its purpose continues to evolve.

Vision matters

The word vision comes from the Latin word videre, which means "to see," but it's about much more than passive observation. A vision describes not what is, but what could be. It embodies leaders' aspirations for what their organization will look like at a given point, and it prevents them – and their colleagues – from slipping into short-term thinking. Having a vision is essential for enabling two-directional thinking, a key element of escaping the short-term trap.

An effective vision is a tangible, immediate way to give direction to an organization's future, particularly in periods of change and uncertainty, when maintaining the status quo is unlikely to create success. It should also be vivid and inspiring, as part of its job is to unite others behind it so that the whole organization can move in the same direction. It should also be aspirational enough to challenge and stretch the company, and specific enough to be used to focus and prioritize activities.

Most companies do not have effective visions, at least if we trust that their written statements are an accurate representation of reality. For a start, a large number of statements are generic in their breadth and perspective, lack any distinguishing features, and demonstrate absolutely no perspective on the future. Vision statements along the lines of "We want to be the leader in our industry" have all these flaws plus the added bonus of inbuilt obsolescence given the way in which traditional industry boundaries are breaking down and cross-industry competition is increasing.

An effective vision requires having a point of view about the future, looking beyond today's environment. It also requires developing a point of view on what it will take to succeed in this emerging world, not just continuing with what the firm does today. Some of the best genuine vision statements we unearthed during our research were not the formal outlines published on websites or in reports. Instead, they were descriptions that characterized the business that the organization will pursue in in the future.

A new vision for a new playing field: Nestlé

Nestlé's website describes its vision and values as: "Nestlé's objectives are to be recognised as the world leader in Nutrition, Health and Wellness, trusted by all its stakeholders, and to be the reference for financial performance in its industry."

This vision was created a little over a decade ago when Peter Brabeck-Letmathe, then the company's CEO, decided to reposition the business as more than a food and drink company. The change in vision, once accepted by the board, also required considerable changes to the business itself, including rethinking R&D and restructuring nutrition. "And we are still in this process," said Brabeck-Letmathe, who is now the company's chairman. "We are not yet where we think we have to be."

This vision has helped to reshape the direction and activities of the whole business. The first stage in its transformation involved shifting its focus from the products themselves to how they are prepared and consumed, and increasing the emphasis on nutrition.

Current CEO Paul Bulcke firmly aligned the entire Nestlé organization behind this nutrition, health, and wellness vision, and together with Nestlé chairman Peter Brabeck-Letmathe, shifted the company's emphasis further. In doing so the company has entered a new playing field of opportunities that sits between the traditional food and pharmaceutical industries. That movement came about partly because the company recognized the potential impact of some of the trends discussed in the last chapter. For example, chronic disease is increasing to the point where it could reduce world GDP by as much as 3% by 2015; health care costs in the U.S. could rise from 15% to 29% of GDP; and health care expenditure in China, Russia and India could increase to a collective total of US$1 trillion by 2015. (Source: Nestlé). The company's vision was refined based on this perspective of its changing playing field and a belief that treating sick people is no longer a sustainable approach to global health care. Rather, there needs to be a new focus on personalized health, science, and nutrition to keep people healthier, longer.

Nestlé has continued to launch new businesses and investments aligned with its vision. An important move was the establishment of the Nestlé Health Science Company as a 100% subsidiary and the creation of the Nestlé Institute of Health Sciences. In these and other activities, Nestlé is preparing the internal capabilities, mindset and relationships to fundamentally alter its relationship with its consumers in line with its vision.

At the same time as making these and other changes, it has maintained strong discipline in its core businesses to ensure that they maintain operational efficiency and keep up to date with changing consumer trends.

In other words, Nestlé's vision is helping it to bridge the gap.

The vision itself has a number of interesting characteristics that make that possible. First, it is built on a thought-through understanding of the future and an analysis of what it will take for the company to be successful in the future, not on a reboot of what made it successful in the past. Second, its focus is not limited by traditional industry or market boxes. And third, it addresses the root cause of challenges facing the company (commoditization of food and drink production) by recognizing that people want to be healthy and well, not just fed.

Another important aspect of the vision is that it has created a path, not a fixed point. It forms part of the foundation that the company and its leaders need to be able to identify and evaluate options over time, and recognizes that a big part of preparing for the future is being constantly aware that things can change. This characteristic also enables two-directional thinking: it helps leaders to see both what they need to do to strengthen the business today, and what they need to do today to build the skills, capabilities, and resources needed to realize that vision in the future.

What role should vision play in preparing an organization for the future?

Reliable crystal balls are in short supply. An effective vision is the best substitute available. It will not let leaders see the future, but it will make the way a little less cloudy. Its main role here, in fact, is making sure that leaders do not let uncertainty hold them back.

Developing an effective vision requires work. It requires rethinking your playing field and then it requires leaders to consider, and make choices, on what it will take to succeed in the future.

Informed choice, based on rethinking the playing field, is better than no choice, just as much of the value in any decision-making process is the learning along the way. A vision is not a fortune-teller's prediction that is either right or wrong about the future; it is a set of choices that leaders and their leadership teams make, based on their assumptions and understanding of where the world will be, and what their role will be in that world. That is, it should be based on the point of view they developed when rethinking their playing field; a vision that considers only one company, and not the broader context, is no vision at all.

And, because that vision is of the company's position in the future, it enables two-directional thinking: in addition to just addressing immediate issues, leaders can work back from it to the present so that they can identify the additional changes needed now to prepare for the future.

An effective vision plays two important roles inside an organization in preparing it for the future: supporting alignment and enabling focus and prioritization.

Supporting alignment Managers, professionals, and workers all tend to see their employer through their own particular lens, which shapes how they see and react to opportunities, problems, and ideas. It can also mean that people in different parts of the same organization can have dramatically different views of what the company should be doing – or even, sometimes, what it is doing.

Ask the executive who runs manufacturing how the company should improve, and she will tell you: "If only we got better at manufacturing, we could do this, and this, and this." Over in finance, however, someone else is looking at the numbers and saying to himself: "You know, we could really get ahead if we improved cash flow," while in the office next door the marketing director is telling her team about the exciting new direction things will take when her next campaign is launched. This lack of alignment, starting from the top, can pull an organization apart, especially down in the organization, where these different silos have to interact.

A coherent shared vision can help address this. It is not a silver bullet, by any means – creating a vision and engaging the entire organization behind it is hard – but it will go a long way towards addressing the issues. A vision allows people to see where the company as a whole is going, and then shape the agenda for their particular part of it. However, a vision will not do much good if members of the leadership team are the only people who know what it is, believe in it, and act upon it.

Shared properly, a vision is a powerful way of uniting organizations and focusing employees' efforts. The contrast with companies without such alignment is sharp: in these, each business unit, or even each individual team, does what it thinks is needed to go where it thinks the business should go. This results, as you can imagine – perhaps even as you have seen – in organizations degenerating into a series of silos that move in different, even contradictory, directions.

A shared vision also allows decision-making to occur at company rather than silo level, which ensures that the trade-offs and choices that are a necessary part of such processes are always made with the big picture in mind.

Enabling focus and prioritization The vision should reflect the specific and informed choices that an organization's leadership makes about its direction. As such it plays an important role in ensuring focus and prioritization within an organization by clarifying the direction in which the leaders of a company have decided to move in the future.

Preparing for the future often requires fundamental change that takes time to accomplish, but lengthy processes can be vulnerable to all sorts of forces that can knock them off track or shift their focus. An effective vision, working in conjunction with a clear purpose, provides a firm yardstick by which activities can be assessed, prioritized, and directed.

It assists focus in much the same way: by providing a firm point that makes it easier to sift out root causes from the distracting chaff of other pressures, which in turn enables concentration on necessary fundamental changes. This also assists leadership teams to identify the longer-term issues that need addressing.

Thinking in scenarios: how to craft an effective vision

An effective vision needs to be grounded in your point of view on the future, but it should be developed by harnessing and stretching the experience and creativity of your organization, and perhaps even its stakeholders. Involving people with different perspectives both from inside and outside the organization is important. This is where thinking in scenarios can help.

Many executives attempting to develop visions struggle. Often, their efforts are simple straight-line continuations of what they do now, projected into the future. Even those who have tried to rethink their playing field can find it difficult to bring the resulting insights to bear in a way that truly breaks free of short-term thinking.

The easiest way to escape this trap is for leaders, and their leadership teams, to explore multiple alternatives – multiple visions of the future, if you like – and to consider the implications of each choice. Investigating multiple possibilities will allow leaders to more clearly understand and identify the choices that need to be made.

At least some of the alternatives put up for discussion should look at the extremes of possibility. It is also important that scenario thinking is not simply about changing the variables that leaders cannot control, such as energy prices, but about those that are within their remit. The whole point is discovering what leaders can and should change, not simply how they should react.

• •

Perspectives from the front line: vision

Feike Sijbesma DSM's mission and vision is described in two sentences: *"Our purpose is to create brighter lives for people today and generations to come"* and *"We connect our unique competences in life sciences and materials sciences to create solutions that nourish, protect and improve performance."*

When Feike Sijbesma, the company's CEO, talked to us about his vision, he said: *"We look at the issues facing the world. Based on these we developed a strategy, a direction. And we hold firmly to that: staying the course. Our values are key in the way we implement our strategy. And since in our case this resulted in a transformation of our company we needed not only to adjust our portfolio but also our culture and leadership style."*

Taking this into account, he continued: *"We are much more than a chemical, or nowadays a life sciences and materials sciences company. We transformed the company, but a key part of that transformation is improving things for the people on this planet and the planet itself, not just the business alone."*

Matti Alahuhta At Kone, the website describes the elevator and escalator company's vision in these words: *"Kone's vision is to create the best People Flow™ experience. Our strategy is to deliver a performance edge to our customers by creating the best user experience with innovative People Flow™ solutions. Simultaneously, our people leadership and processes enable operational excellence and cost competitiveness."*

"People Flow™ focuses Kone's attention on the last, and often most difficult part of many trips. Kone's products are found in offices and in crowded spaces, where moving people can be a very negative experience. Kone's vision is thus focused not just on its products and services, but how to improve this experience for people moving through these crowded environments.

"Kone is guided by this vision," said the elevator company's CEO, Matti Alahuhta. *"Our desire is that one day, all the millions of people who use our products and services will think to themselves 'this is how great life can be' moving even in the crowded and rushed environments in which we operate."*

• •

Ask yourself: have you redefined your vision?

An effective vision clarifies the direction in which you and your organization should move, based on how you see its future playing field. As such, it drives choices and focus through the organization, guiding every day decisions and aligning people behind the company's ambition.

Ask yourself:

Remember rethinking What opportunities and challenges will be created by changes in your playing field? How does your vision reflect this?

Choice What explicit choices have you made in defining your vision? What transformational changes will be needed to pursue it – that you need to start making today?

Guide How can your vision help to guide everyday decision making? Does everyone in your organization know and buy into it?

• •

Redefining success: what gets measured gets done

Metrics are where the rubber hits the road.

What organizations choose to measure, and how they choose to measure it, has an enormous effect on what their people do and how they do it. If employees get promoted or rewarded for hitting certain targets, for example, they will prioritize their activities in a way that lets them do this.

This is why leaders need to be extremely careful to define success in a way that aligns with their company's purpose and vision. If they do not, they will end up with metrics that skew its path, or even prevent it from moving forward. Leaders must define success in a way that reflects and supports their preparations for the future, and develop metrics that measure this effectively.

This is not easy. It is certainly not as straightforward as identifying metrics that shape and drive short-term actions – which are also, of course, necessary. It is, however, a critical part of preparing an organization for a volatile and uncertain future. The key – part of bridging the gap – is to have the right balance of metrics focused on delivering today and preparing for the longer term, then to ensure that they are not misapplied.

Short-term metrics can destroy long-term opportunities

Leaders who want to kill long-term investments should measure and manage them using the same logic and approach that they use when evaluating and managing well-established businesses.

Measuring an established business will typically focus on immediate operational and financial targets such as revenue, cost, and profit, but the measures of success for long-term investments are more often around learning and developing options that will lead to future success. This means that leaders must find or create metrics that account for differences in the nature of activities, as well as their objectives, and their focus. They should also reflect the holistic challenges of preparing an organization for the future.

This does not mean, however, that all existing tools must be discarded. Balanced scorecards, "big hairy audacious goals," and the triple bottom line can all be useful, as long as they are applied in a way that helps the organization to focus on long-term transformational issues in everyday decision making, as well as today's performance. Again, balance is critical. Whatever metrics leaders select must be holistic, not siloed KPIs, and must be matched with an active management process to ensure that they are actually used to drive accountability.

Measuring preparation for the future

Measuring an organization's readiness for the future has to happen in two dimensions. The first should consider internal and external readiness, and any fundamental changes this requires. Internally, this may mean significant shifts in capabilities, business models, and mindsets, for example when moving from being a food and drink company to one focused on personal wellbeing, or from being a telecom company to a lifestyle company.

External readiness needs to be considered in the light of falling industry boundaries, changes in stakeholder expectations, and the shifting relationship between business and society. This requires leaders to have a clear understanding of who those stakeholders are and how they relate to their organization; Mike Brown's story, which we tell below, offers one effective approach to this. At both ends of the spectrum, metrics should reflect these major shifts.

The second dimension can be characterized as "heads" and "hearts." Rational readiness – the heads end of the spectrum – relates to the organization's core structural factors, while emotional readiness – hearts – is determined by its ability to engage others, inside and outside the company, in its activities.

Putting the two dimensions together in the diagram below highlights the four areas an organization needs to measure and monitor as it builds readiness for the future, raising specific questions for which metrics can be established.

Measuring readiness for the future: A framework

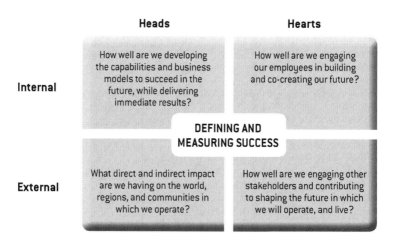

	Heads	**Hearts**
Internal	How well are we developing the capabilities and business models to succeed in the future, while delivering immediate results?	How well are we engaging our employees in building and co-creating our future?
	DEFINING AND MEASURING SUCCESS	
External	What direct and indirect impact are we having on the world, regions, and communities in which we operate?	How well are we engaging other stakeholders and contributing to shaping the future in which we will operate, and live?

Internal, Heads Metrics here should assess the speed and effectiveness with which the business is developing the capabilities and business models needed to position itself in line with its vision. These are likely to incorporate measures of efficiency, flexibility, speed, capability, and financial strength. They may also include measures of progress in optimizing current business activities, as it is easier for leaders to free up time and resources to focus on long-term preparations when short-term operations are running smoothly.

The good news is that these types of metrics are concrete, which means that they are generally easy to identify and track. The bad news is that this means they often get the majority of management's attention. The short-term measures are the easiest of all to manage, which – if the focus on these areas detracts from others – can hold organizations even more firmly in the short-term trap.

Internal, Hearts The measures of success in this quadrant should reflect the need to define and monitor progress in cultural and mindset issues. Questions that need to be answered include: Do people know where we are going? Do they buy into it? Do they believe in the purpose and values we espouse? Are they willing to make the fundamental changes needed to succeed in the future?

Changing the way people work is one of the hardest, most critical, and slowest aspects of any change process. Milestones and metrics can help organizations keep an eye on how fast they are progressing in this regard, and whether or not they are staying on track. These metrics are likely to cover areas such as employee engagement, corporate culture, employer reputation, employee turnover, the talent pipeline, and employees' motivation and commitment.

External, Heads The third quadrant focuses attention on the impact that the organization has both directly and indirectly on the world at large, as well as the regions and communities within which it operates. Relevant metrics are likely to cover areas such as sustainability, environmental impact, and contribution to education, employment, and health in local communities. Unilever's Sustainable Living Plan, which we outlined earlier in the book, offers a good example of what such metrics can look like.

External, Hearts Here, too, the focus is the outside world, but in this case the emphasis is on the emotional engagement aspects of the organization's relationships with its stakeholders, as well as on how it will contribute to shaping the future. Metrics here could include external stakeholder perceptions of the company, breadth and depth of external networks, corporate reputation, and involvement in partnerships with other organizations.

Tailoring metrics to stakeholders: Nedbank Group

Mike Brown, the CEO of Nedbank Group, one of the biggest banks in South Africa, defines success very broadly.

"We've expressed a vision of the organization, which is that we want to build Africa's most admired bank, by our staff, by our customers, by our shareholders, by our regulators, and by the communities within which we operate," he said.

He lists those five stakeholder groups in that order very deliberately. Many of the mistakes made in organizations around the world occur because they put shareholders at the top of the stakeholder list – and, in some cases, fail to include anyone else on that list at all.

"In the U.S., some of that is because of the legal system," he said. "The obligations of the board in the U.S. are to the shareholders; in South Africa the obligations of the board are in fact to the company and all of its stakeholders, of which the shareholders are one – a very important one, but they're just one."

Brown's starting position is that the bank cannot provide a superior service to its customers unless its employees are energized, motivated, and adhere to its culture and values. "And if we don't provide our customers with superior service, we'll never provide our shareholders with superior returns," he said. "So for us, it goes staff, customers, shareholders, regulators, and communities.

"The right staff operating within the right culture offers the business a real competitive advantage in a sector where all banks tend to offer much the same products and services to customers," he said.

"We've invested a lot of money – and continue to do so – on personal mastery which is about understanding your impact on other people, including thinking carefully before you talk or act. EQ is as important as IQ. There are so many careless individual actions that can cause a huge amount of damage to any organization."

Next on the list are clients, which rated Nedbank three out of four for retail service and two out of four in wholesale in a survey. Brown and his team now have a "major focus" on how the bank can lift its service position with clients.

Shareholder satisfaction is relatively easy to measure thanks to visible metrics such as price to book ratios that allow comparison with your peers. "We were the lowest a year ago – our ratio was 1.5 while others were around 1.8 – so we absolutely want to close that gap. We've done all the analyses as to what we think causes it, and we've got all the metrics and strategies around trying to fix it."

Then come regulators. "I haven't seen any other bank in the world that has being admired by regulators in its vision statement, but we've had ours in there for a while now. And just what did the global financial crisis tell so many banks?

Unless you pay proper attention to your regulators, if you're going to get caught out somewhere, who are you going to go to for help? The same people that you were not paying sufficient attention to. So the regulators are very important in our lives because we operate under the fact that they've given us a license to be a bank – and they have the license to take it back. As a bank you're a zero unless you look after that constituency properly."

Finally, communities. Nedbank does "a huge amount" around payroll giving and staff volunteering to fix crèches, clean up rivers, and support HIV hospitals together with a focus on education, community development and job creating in its corporate social investment programs. "This is fantastic for the communities, but it's also great from a team-building perspective inside the organization," Brown said.

"So at the end of the day, if you look at how we measure things, while the financial side is very important and drives the size of incentive pools, you have to hit your scores on all the other stuff – staff, customers, regulators, and communities – to be sustainable and be rewarded."

Perspectives from the front line: success

Andrew Coulsen The CEO of Dimension Data Europe, which has achieved a cumulative annual growth rate of 35% in earnings before tax and interest for the last five years, told us: *"You get what you inspect, not what you expect. You need to set measures for both the short and long terms and there need to be common rules for all, so no matter what level everyone wins or loses with similar guiding metrics. This drives a consistent focus across the business. You also have to manage the consequences consistently and fairly, which means setting clear expectations at the outset."*

Anand Mahindra The Mahindra Group's chairman has a very personal definition of business success, albeit one that is also partnered with clear metrics. *"Ten years from now, I want the Mahindra name to generate a positive reaction. I would like people to say, 'What a great company.' Not because it's the largest or the most profitable, but because the company* *really makes them wish there were more companies like Mahindra.*

"To do this we need to bring alive our no-limits philosophy. Here wishy-washy nice words won't work. We have a very rigorous performance management system in place. But what gives us the extra edge is the portfolio of choices that have been made according to our purpose."

Mike Brown *"What worries me every day as a leader is what I am doing to make sure that I leave behind an organization that is sustainably better than the one I inherited,"* said the Nedbank CEO. *"To me, that's the measure of success. So what worries me is not just delivery of this year's targets – we have lots of plans to make sure we do this. But the issues for me are what are we doing around building the new businesses and new products that will make us money in the years ahead?"*

• •

Ask yourself: have you redefined your metrics?

The four lenses introduced in the diagram above provide a broad view of what organizational success in the future could look like, and should help you to translate your company's purpose and vision statements into concrete measures and targets that can be used to shape decision making and action both for today and the long term.

Ask yourself:

Balance Are your metrics properly balanced between internal, external, rational, and emotional measures of success? If not, where are the gaps between rational (heads) and emotional (hearts) measures of success to be able to assess how well we are preparing for the future?

Relevance Do these metrics clearly reflect your purpose and vision for the future of the organization?

Communication Have you shared these metrics with key stakeholders inside and outside the company? Have you ensured that they are engaged with the metrics and aligned with the goals you want to pursue?

• •

Redefine your ambition: recap

Purpose matters An organization's purpose explains why it exists. Redefine that purpose, and you can redefine the nature of that organization – exactly the sort of fundamental change that may be needed when preparing for the future.

A clear purpose helps leaders to rethink their playing field without holding on to the past, which in turn helps them develop a perspective on the future. It also provides structure and clarity when making decisions about the business's direction.

Finally, a well-expressed purpose will help stakeholders understand what they can expect from organizations and their leaders – something that is important in a connected world, where relationships are critical for success.

Vision matters Vision is an exciting, inspiring picture of what the company could be. An effective vision is not a prediction made with a crystal ball, but a compelling destination built on a clear purpose and a perspective of the future. It helps organizations to focus and prioritize their activities by showing them the path ahead, and it supports alignment by giving everyone a clear sense of where the company wants to go.

Redefining success: what gets measured gets done Metrics that are aligned with an organization's purpose and vision will enhance its progress, but all too often companies measure success in ways that skew what they are trying to achieve. This has particular implications when preparing for the future, as attempting to assess long-term planning using short-term metrics will almost always end badly.

Redefining your ambition requires leaders to confront four key challenges:

1. Define or redefine your company's purpose and vision, and then bring them to life inside and outside the company.

2. Have the courage to stand up to financial markets by developing and realizing a long-term ambition, rather than accepting their short-term agenda. Align how you define and use metrics with the direction of the company.

3. Turn internal skepticism into aligned ownership and commitment. Define acceptable and unacceptable behaviors.

4. Gain the support of the board and other key stakeholders.

Rethink Your Playing Field challenges leaders to look at how the world is changing, and from there to take a point of view on the future. Redefining is about how to use that point of view as a foundation for shaping a clearly-defined purpose and vision, and creating effective metrics for success. These elements will play a critical part in your organization's preparedness for the future, as well as in guiding the practical changes covered in the next chapter, Reshape How You Work.

Measure your progress

Use the following table to assess where you are today in terms of readiness to redefine your ambition. As before, key ideas introduced in this chapter are in the shaded rows of text, while column 1 describes the least advanced and 5 describes the most advanced state of practice in companies today. Options 2 or 4 mean your company is somewhere in between each state of practice. Go through this assessment twice: once from your organization's perspective, and once from your own personal position. Have others in your senior leadership team – as well as people lower down the organization, and even your broader stakeholders – complete the exercise independently to gain additional insights.

1	2	3	4	5
Role of purpose				
Our purpose is just words on a wall; we're here to make money		We build stakeholder relationships for mutual benefit; we have focused partnerships to address topics of mutual interest		Our purpose shapes the markets in which we choose to operate, our core activities, and ways of working
Role of vision				
Our vision is just words on a wall; we will deal with the future in the future – we're busy		Our vision stretches our thinking about our current business; it helps to reshape current activities primarily in existing markets		Our vision provides a point of view on the future around all stakeholder needs; it helps redefine the business, capabilities, and ways of working we need to be fit for the future
Making choices, taking actions				
Our purpose and vision have no impact on daily decision-making or action		Our purpose and vision are used to check our decisions and to guide our choices, in most cases, but generally at the top of the organization		Our purpose and vision are the key drivers for all decision-making; they enable and empower our employees at all levels to take action

1	2	3	4	5
Definition and use of metrics				
The only relevant metric is profit		We use double or triple bottom line approaches, but financials come first		Our metrics are holistic, internal and external, and hearts and heads, helping us to redefine value and step beyond the triple bottom line to shape the direction of our company
Alignment and communications				
It's simple: everybody knows that profit is our sole purpose, vision and metric		Our leaders have a good understanding of our purpose, vision and metrics; we have some communications across the broader organization, but there is not complete understanding and alignment at all levels		All our employees and stakeholders have a good understanding of our purpose, vision and metrics and what this means for each of them; this drives daily activities and alignment behind our ambition

FOUR: Reshape How You Work

Executives are busy, as we said; so too are the organizations they lead. Some are even approaching the point of exhaustion as they attempt to fight the many challenges facing businesses today.

Unfortunately, many executives also spend a significant amount of time on tasks and activities they feel do not add value to their organization. They know this perfectly well – according to our informal survey, executives estimate they spend a third or more of their time on these non-value adding activities – but they cannot see any way to change the balance.

When we ask them why they spend so much time on tasks that do not add value, they tell us that they have no choice. Someone else in the organization, often at headquarters, has instructed them to do it, and they do not feel able to refuse.

Leaders who have redefined their ambition, as covered in the last chapter, have the potential advantage of having an objective, a future goal, that can help them to create their own agenda to help prioritize what they do today. Leaders who do not have their own agendas can become the victims of the agendas of others.

But this recognition and agenda alone will not bring about the concrete changes needed to prepare an organization for the future. Until these changes happen, all the work done with the first two Rs is little more than a nice intellectual exercise.

Leaders have to take the step that moves all this thinking from theory to practice: they must reshape how they, and their organizations, work. This means translating the understanding and insights gathered in the thinking part of this process into action. It most definitely does not mean adding tasks to the bottom of a long to-do list; these actions are all about what will add value, what will move things forward, what will prepare the organization for long-term, sustainable success.

New ways of working are needed if organizations are to succeed in both delivering results today and preparing for the future.

Remember that preparing for the future typically requires fundamental change, not incremental improvement. Reshaping how a company works means overcoming assumptions that were instrumental to past success, but which can limit its ability in the future. Many organizations fail when they allow their core business models and mindsets to get in the way of innovation. Others fall into the same busyness trap that catches individual executives: they are far too busy to make time to think about change, even though the tasks occupying their time are not really getting them anywhere, let alone addressing the root causes of issues for the future.

Old approaches to working in our new world do little to inspire others, either. As one of our interviewees put it, leaders can't motivate an organization by continually restructuring Belgium.

Finding new approaches to how you work covers three main areas. The first is clarifying and building alignment around the organization's agenda: how it prioritizes activity, how it develops strategies, budgets, and plans, and how it balances the need for what we call sprints and marathons. The second is reshaping interactions with stakeholders, which need to shift from being simple transactional arrangements to genuine, ongoing relationships. The third involves changing ways of working, moving from accepting complacency to creating the courage, commitment, and capacity to challenge and move the organization forward. Finally there is a fourth area, specifically for CEOs, associated with the relationship between the senior executives and their companies' owners and boards.

Build your agenda: balance sprints and marathons

Throughout this book we have looked at the notion of two-directional thinking: the idea that organizations cannot afford to define their priorities based solely on their current situation, because this will make it impossible to escape the short-term trap. Instead companies need to define them by looking forward from the present and back from the expected future at the same time. This allows the balance between short-term and long-term thinking needed to bridge the gap between present results and long-term success.

Leaders need to use two-directional thinking throughout the reshaping process, including when they plan, budget, and strategize, to identify both sprints, which accelerate immediate actions and priorities, and marathons, which drive transformational change. As we will describe, sprints and marathons form the foundation for continuous reshaping.

Stop misusing budgets, plans, and strategies

Here you may say we already have processes in place to shape and define our agenda. We have detailed planning and budgeting processes. The reality is, however, that today at most companies these processes lock them into the short-term trap and do not contribute to preparing for the future.

Budgets, plans, and strategies are essential tools in shaping activities in an organization. Used correctly, they can help leaders to clarify their agendas, define and balance priorities, and shape the activities that move an organization forward. But more often than not they are not used effectively.

A large part of the problem stems from a fairly basic misuse or misunderstanding of the tools themselves. People think that they understand them, perhaps because they have studied them at business school as well as using them every day, but our experience suggests that this is not the case.

Very often executives who claim to be thinking strategically are actually practicing tactical, short-term thinking. In stable markets this is not a particularly serious issue, but in a world of constant, significant change, this approach can make it very difficult to escape the lure of short-termism, particularly as pressure grows to meet budgets and short-term targets.

The best starting point for leaders preparing to reshape how they work, then, is a quick refresher course in how each of these tools differ, and when they are most appropriate.

Budgets, plans, and strategies: definitions

	Budgets	Plans	Strategies
Time horizon	1 year	2-3 years	5 years +
Playing field	Defined targets	Defined boundaries	Framing opportunities
Process focus	Setting concrete metrics for performance measurement	Rigorously analyzing products, markets, and functions	Defining options, selecting a path
Mindset	Delivery on commitments	"What CAN we do"; fix problems, avoid failures	"What MUST we do"; learn, adjust, lead
Issue frame	Execution to achieve targets	Systematic analysis, data driven	Constructive dialog, data enabled
View of change	Interference, cost	Painful temporary process	Continuous necessity
Success metrics	Budgets	Milestones, targets	Institutional strength
Key risk	Missing targets	Misjudging boundaries and trends	Deciding too late

Budgets Budgets are all about delivering on immediate commitments. Their focus is concrete targets set within a tightly defined world – often internal – and a limited time frame of a year or less. The primary mindset is one of avoiding mistakes and hitting targets: sticking to a budget means success, missing one equals failure, both personally and organizationally. There is a strong emphasis on predictability and consistency, so change is often viewed as interference, or a source of additional cost.

Budgets also drive immediate behavior shifts. A company that it is falling behind on its budgetary milestones may demand that all units step up performance or reduce costs until things are back on track, for example. Fear of missing targets – the biggest risk in the budgetary world – can lead to companies and executives dedicating significant amounts of time to overcoming shortfalls.

Plans The key characteristic here is rigorous analysis, which is used to set targets within defined existing business boundaries, although over a longer time frame than with budgets; the planning process typically involves setting product, functional, and market objectives and activities over a two to three year period. Planning does not look beyond the boundaries that define a firm's current activities. The process often combines top-down and bottom-up approaches to cover both target setting and how to hit those targets through incremental adjustments to existing activities.

Executives often use data analysis to identify areas for immediate improvement when planning. The focus tends to be on what the company can accomplish in the time under consideration, with a particular emphasis on addressing problems and enhancing short-term achievements. The result of planning is the establishment of concrete targets and milestones for the period under review.

During the planning process, change is often viewed as a temporary annoyance that must be endured before things get back to normal. Few executives plan from the perspective that change is the norm, not the exception.

One of the biggest dangers with planning is that inaccurate assumptions about the future can creep into the picture. Such assumptions, which are often based on historic performance and perspectives rather than a grasp of the trends shaping the new playing fields, can play a big part in setting up companies to hold on to the past.

The other big challenge is ensuring that planning is a dynamic process. The ever-increasing speed of change means that plans can become outdated faster than ever, so finding a new way to approach planning is critical.

Strategy The focus here should be on the big picture and the long term. It should be on how leaders define their company's path, and build options for the future. It should be on how an institution shapes and achieves its long-term overall aims, and stands in contrast with tactics, which focus on short-term actions and success.

This does not mean that a strategy should, or even can, set out exactly where the company must be in a decade's time. Executives who believe that they can predict the future with the detail and accuracy required for this are fooling themselves. What it does mean is that the strategy keeps its focus on pursuing success in the long term, based on developing insights and understanding about the direction of future change.

Change will always create new opportunities and challenges, and organizations – and their strategies – must be flexible enough to grasp them, without becoming purely reactive. As such, strategy is about framing opportunities and defining options, not working within predetermined boundaries. It is about proactive anticipation, not defensive reaction. As one CEO told us: "When you have no options, you have no future."

Strategic thinking requires leadership teams to move beyond the "what can we do" mindset. Frankly, markets, consumers, and competitors don't care what you can or cannot do; if you can't do something, someone else will, and they will win. The mindset should be "what must we do to be successful in the future," as this will allow strategy to be used to identify, and make explicit choices about, the options available.

The need for judgment and adaptability means that strategy requires leadership and choice, not simple data management or a revamp of what has worked in the past. It also demands that leaders understand that change is a continuous necessity, not a disruption or an added cost, as it so often is during budgeting and planning. Strategies must ensure that organizations change at least as fast as the environments in which they operate, or they will unavoidably fall behind.

With this in mind, the biggest risk when developing strategy is starting the change process too late. Fundamentally reshaping an organization takes time, not least because it is likely to require the development of new skills and capabilities as well as new ways of thinking. Leaders who hang on to the past for too long may well find themselves caught without the time they need to bring about the changes that they have identified when they do finally get around to making those strategic choices.

Finally, a strategy will define a variety of KPIs and milestones that allow executives to keep track of progress, but the ultimate measure of its performance is whether or not the organization is better prepared for long-term, sustainable success.

Each tool has its place

The outline above is not intended as a criticism of budgets or plans. These are important tools, and leaders need to know how – and, critically, when – to use them. Many organizations get themselves into a muddle because they develop their budgets, plans, and strategies in the wrong order. They should start with strategy, use that to frame their plans, and then use both to develop budgets that support the overall strategy.

All too often, however, we see companies attempting to build a strategy using short-term operational targets – part of budgeting – as a foundation. In other cases, they try to develop growth strategies around traditional categories such as products and markets, which are actually part of their planning framework.

Strategy must be developed before planning and budgets come into the picture, because it defines the overall path by which the company will reach its ambition. It should be based on the vision and purpose that leaders redefined with their rethought playing field in mind; basing it on existing budgets or plans is a surefire way to design a strategy that will help hold on to the past.

Once the strategy is in place, plans, which are narrower in focus and outline the steps along the way, come next. Budgets, which set the limits within which actions must be executed and keep things on track, are the final stage. Leaders who reverse the order are starting the process by putting themselves into boxes rather than breaking them down. So, use strategy to define the path to your future ambition, planning to define your boundaries, and budgeting to define your targets.

Two-directional thinking: identifying sprints and marathons

Companies that base their activities on historical assumptions and activities – essentially meaning that change is only ever a series of incremental steps from the past – will always be reactive, never proactive, when dealing with the changes that the future throws at them. Leaders who want to overcome this need to bring two-directional thinking back in to play. In this context, two-directional thinking involves identifying and balancing sprints and marathons.

Using two-directional thinking to identify sprints and marathons

Sprints Most companies have a host of unresolved issues and nonproductive activities taking up valuable time and effort in the present. These issues are frequently well known, but resolving them tends to drag on. Often they are important for strengthening the current business foundation, for example because they take waste out of what an organization does today to free up time and resources for other important issues. However, some are not.

Leaders need to identify and deal with these issues without delay, because organizations have neither the time nor the resources to hold on to things from the past that add no value to either the present or the future.

This is where sprints come in: they are the activities that must be accelerated to address issues today, and to address them quickly, to ensure that the company has a strong foundation from which to drive future success. If a company has a three year plan to resolve these issues, for example, it needs to shorten the timeframe to one to two years.

Marathons The other elements of the agenda highlighted in two-directional thinking are the marathons: long, difficult, and demanding of stamina. Typical marathons involve issues such as changing corporate culture or building a new organizational capability. Organizations may start marathons today, but they do so because their perspective on the future shows them that they have to do that to get where they want to be in many years' time. This means acknowledging that it will take them a considerable time to reach the finish line, and that they will need to put in sustained effort throughout if they are not to fall by the wayside.

Sprints and marathons fit in to strategy, planning, and budgeting in different ways. The need for a sprint tends to be identified during the planning or budgeting stage, because that is when companies are most likely to pick up on issues that are taking up time and resources that could be better spent preparing for the future.

Marathons, by contrast, are inherently part of the longer-term transformation agenda, so they tend to fall into the domain of strategy and planning. Typically the need for a marathon will be identified during strategy preparation, when companies are defining where they want to go and what they need to do to get there, while the planning stage will bring the marathon in to the "here and now" agenda.

Ask yourself: can you tackle sprints and marathons?

Effective use of strategy, plans, and budgets will enable you to create an agenda that reflects the challenges of delivering today while preparing your organization for the future. Identifying and focusing on sprints and marathons will allow you to create the basis for action.

Ask yourself:

Sprints What are the biggest issues and activities on which you spend time and resources today? Are they moving your organization in the direction you want to go? If not, what will it take to resolve these issues fast so that you can free up resources to prepare for the future? These are your sprints.

Marathons Look back to today from your vision of the future. In what areas must you transform your business? These are your marathons. Are you allocating sufficient time, resources, and management focus to these areas today, to be able to move forward at the right speed?

Balance How can you shift the focus and efforts arising from your strategy, planning, and budgeting processes to achieve a balanced agenda of sprints and marathons?

• •

Move from transactions to creative relationships

The second topic area we address in reshaping how you work involves how you interact with others, inside and outside the organization.

Relationships will be central to success in the future. In a world defined by networks and connections it is no longer possible to rely on one-off transactions to define what we do and how we do it. Few companies, if any, will be able to meet the expectations of all their stakeholders by working alone.

In a transactional mindset, which dominates most interactions today, each party is independent and both parties seek to gain power or benefit by making the other dependent on it. For example, employees work for employers and the employer has the power. Consumers purchase products, while businesses try to create dependence and power – and thus profit – by creating loyalty, building barriers to switching, or offering incentives to continue buying their products. Owners exert power by demanding high short-term returns, while societies use laws as a source of power.

But such transactional relationships are no longer sustainable. The days of independent control are giving way to a new world of interdependent influence, across all relationships.

It will take effective, meaningful relationships to build bridges to the future and it will take genuine, open dialog to build those partnerships. When business is about connections, how those connections are made, and maintained, matters.

Despite this, most companies cling to traditional views of business: you do something for me, and I will give you something in return. This transactional attitude pervades all interactions, whether they are with consumers, suppliers, employees, or any other group. At its heart is a firm-centered, short-term view of the world in which the underlying question is always "How can I get the most out of this right now?" In this view, success is about maintaining control and, ultimately, hitting the next set of targets.

But this view is wrong, and will become increasingly dangerous in the future. Businesses are no longer at the center of value creation; consumers are.

Organizations that move from transactions to relationships will be more flexible and better able to make the most of changes such as the rise of connected communities, while managing the implications of, for example, changing social expectations of business. Companies that insist on sticking to the old ways of doing things will not be prepared for the future.

Real relationships require real engagement

Many companies think that they are already working in partnership with others. Few actually are, at least in the core of their strategy and mindset where it matters most. They may have partnerships in selected activities, but their dominant mindset where it matters most remains transactional.

There is a difference between having a few focused partnerships, such as having CSR-led connections with NGOs or community groups, and building the business based on genuine relationships with stakeholders. Many organizations use relationships as an add-on to current activities, but few use them to define and shape their futures. Having a preferred supplier list or a fair trade policy, for instance, is a long way from having the give and take of a real two-way relationship that can change the company's core activities in terms of its relationship with society, employees, consumers, and others. And talking about a triple bottom line or shared value is all very well, but if the metrics always come second to traditional financial results they are not really shaping the company in any meaningful way.

Effective relationships are based on an active and consistent focus on mutual success. Achieving them requires the implicit acknowledgement that individual firms have much less power to independently control their own destiny than they did in the past. The growth of stakeholder power that we discussed earlier means that businesses will need positive relationships with their stakeholders, including customers, employees, and society more broadly, in order to acquire and maintain the license to operate.

In order to highlight the changes taking place, in the next sections we briefly look at changing relationships with two key stakeholders: consumers and employees. In each area, we then highlight four levels of progress in moving from transactions towards co-creating relationships.

Building the business around consumers

Consumers are changing, as we discussed in Rethink Your Playing Field. They have more power and higher expectations than ever before. Companies need to understand what these expectations are, and how they can meet them, if they are to understand what consumers are willing to pay for. Alongside this, they must understand consumers' increasing desire to engage with companies in a way that is based on factors beyond the characteristics of the products themselves. To do so, firms increasingly need to interact with active communities of consumers.

The traditional starting point has been, and in many cases still is, transactional – level one in the table below. This is a simple arrangement: companies sell their products; consumers buy them. Companies want to understand their consumers well enough to know how to sell them more products, but that's where it stops. Success is measured in sales volume and profit. Changing consumer demand is only relevant in so far as it means tweaking sales and marketing activity.

Growing competition has pushed many organizations up to level two, where relationships are seen as a tool that helps to stabilize and grow sales, and to block competition. Often this means offering a support service alongside a product in a way that broadens the relationship and builds barriers to entry for competitors, but does not change the fundamental producer/seller-consumer/buyer relationship. Success is still defined as increased sales.

Level three, which many organizations are exploring today, involves moving beyond products and services to delivering consumer experiences. Companies at this level get closer to consumers by better understanding their expectations and demands.

Nespresso is a good example of a brand operating at this level. For a start, the company, which sells premium coffee in individual containers, does not characterize its business as selling coffee, but as creating "the ultimate coffee experience." Ignoring traditional category boundaries allows it to think beyond creating a good product – the coffee itself – to consider how consumers make it and how they buy it.

Turning home-brewed coffee into an experience required Nespresso to adapt every stage of its value chain. The coffee is selected from the top 1% of the best grades of coffee available globally. Nespresso partners with farmers to ensure its high-quality supply and also to ensure that its premium prices contribute to farmer development. The coffee is then dried, roasted, ground, and packed at the company's state-of-the-art production facility. A team of coffee experts creates grand cru and limited edition collections, which are offered each season. It constantly creates new designs for specialist coffee machines that brew using Nespresso's aluminum capsules. The company has also expanded its offerings through a vast array of accessories and supplementary products.

As far as relationships with consumers go, the main conduit is the Nespresso Club – the coffee community through which people can buy more coffee capsules, recycle their used pods, find out about special offers, and so on. This has allowed Nespresso to bypass traditional retailers to create direct relationships with more than 8 million coffee consumers. These relationships are supported by its website and an expanding network of global boutique shops.

Nespresso built willingness to pay through its entire purchasing, serving, and consuming experience. It built a desire to engage by addressing issues important to its clients, from sustainable sourcing to direct involvement in innovation, and being part of an elite club.

The result of this approach is remarkable, with sales growing from CHF200 million in 2000 to more than CHF3 billion in 2010. However, the relationship is still ultimately focused on interactions that improve and strengthen the traditional business.

Only a very few companies are actively exploring the fourth level, which is not about adapting current activities around consumer needs but about changing the business itself. Those which are looking at it are doing so in conjunction with the high-level work that they are doing to rethink their playing field, and to redefine their ambition: all three Rs are interlinked. With reshaping, this level thus leads to reinventing markets based on deeper understanding of consumers' holistic and emerging needs, and transforming the business around the consumer.

Tapping into the power of your employees

It is common for leaders to view employees as just another resource input. For many roles, organizational focus is on salary and output, with companies looking for the cheapest sources of labor for defined tasks. Offshoring and outsourcing companies in low-cost locations have grown dramatically based on this level one behavior.

In other organizations, or parts of organizations, the war for talent has encouraged a move to level two. In this case, the focus – for a selection of jobs, at least – shifts from a pure cost/output rationale towards hiring, developing, motivating, and rewarding the best and most capable employees. These companies often like to announce that people are their most important asset; relationships here emphasize employees' loyalty and their contribution to the company in return for salary, benefits, and career opportunities.

This third level of employee relationship typically revolves around highly creative or highly qualified employees, or those from a younger generation. At this level, companies begin to genuinely consider and respond to employees' expectations of their jobs. This attitude is partly driven by recognition that these workers are extremely mobile and perfectly happy to move company if their needs are not being met, and partly by the desire to get the most out of them. These employees want to work for a company that they believe in and where they can have a genuine impact, be it on the organization or on society more broadly. At level three employers have realized that being able to tap in to the passion and commitment of individual employees can work to their benefit, as well as that of the individual.

Reaching this level means breaking away from the limits of traditional job definitions and building commitment and passion in employees so that they want to contribute to the firm's success. One of the biggest challenges is moving ownership of the employee relationship out of the human resources department to the broader leadership of the organization. All leaders should take responsibility for creating the environment that will allow employees to contribute, and the organization to benefit from their activities. All leaders are part of shaping an environment that is attractive and beneficial to demanding employees.

The fourth level of employee relationships, which is more evident in aspiration than in practice, is reached when firms start engaging individual employees in creating the business itself, not just from the top down, but across the entire organization. It gives employees a genuine opportunity to use their entrepreneurial spirit to shape the future of the organization. This next horizon depends on many factors, including alignment, shared ownership of the future direction of the organization, and a willingness to move away from a top-down decision-making process.

Building creative relationships

Relationships will look slightly different for each group of stakeholders, as the table below outlines, but they share three core characteristics in the transition from transactions to collaboration. First, the emphasis shifts from traditional loyalty to active, mutual commitment. Second, conversations become more focused on mutual benefits, with listening, learning, and co-creation on both sides. Third, the partners stop pursuing independence, instead embracing genuine interdependence.

Loyalty is dead, long live commitment What do we mean? Simply that the length of a relationship – the traditional way to measure loyalty – is no longer what matters. What is important today is the quality of that relationship, which is reflected in mutual commitment during that period. Let us explain.

Consumers are switching to private label retail products. Capable, passionate employees switch companies. Traditional joint ventures are facing new challenges as partners pursue their independent interests. Trust in institutions is nearing an all-time low.

From transactional to creative relationships

Level 1: Transactional relationships	Level 2: Extended relationships	Level 3: Balanced relationships	Level 4: Creative relationships
Consumers			
Sell products	Provide products and related services	Deliver consumer experiences	Co-create holistic experiences
Suppliers			
Purchase inputs	Purchase inputs and support services	Supply partnerships	Collaborative problem-solving networks
Employees			
Hire employees	Retain, develop, and motivate employees	Challenge and involve employees	Engage and empower employees
Society			
Meet legal requirements; carry out philanthropic and propaganda activities	Pursue focused partnerships in areas of mutual benefit; CSR as a function	Develop permissible business models; earn the license to operate and grow	Optimize shared value or prosperity
Owners			
Deliver solid financial results	Deliver consistent, predictable results	Expand relations with owners	Attract and expand relations with long-term owners

All of these trends share at least one connection: expectations of relationships with businesses are changing. Stakeholders are no longer satisfied with transactional interactions; they want relationships built on genuine mutual commitment and benefit.

This means that companies, and their leaders, can no longer afford to take others for granted, even if their traditional assumptions about stakeholder roles made this the norm. Consumers, employees, business owners, and society at large all want and expect more understanding and response to their needs, which are growing and changing every day. What is delivered in one period becomes the base for the next year.

These higher expectations come with an increased desire for engagement in the relationships. As we discussed earlier, consumers don't simply want to consume, they want to get involved with innovation and product development.

Employees don't just want jobs that require them to complete defined tasks – they want to find organizations that allow them to add value and contribute to something that has meaning to them. Tapping into this desire for involvement can help to build mutual commitment and significant business benefits.

In a future of growing volatility and uncertainty a company's ability to access the skills, resources, knowledge, and commitment of others will be a significant source of advantage. Developing this ability is not easy. It requires a fundamental shift in thinking, a dramatic increase in openness to others, and a reduction in the not-invented-here mindset.

More than that, it needs leaders to drop their old ideas about loyalty and accept that mutual commitment is the new foundation for sustainable interaction. That is, they need to focus on the ongoing quality of their interactions and relationships with others, not simply how long they last.

From defending to co-creating The second characteristic of moving from transactions to collaborative relationships reflects that good relationships are built on effective two-way communication. This we all know, at least intellectually. But effective communication rarely comes naturally to organizations. Most go through five different stages before they get to where they need to be: dialog that enables co-creation.

The dialog ladder

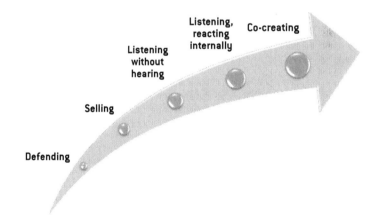

1. *Defending* It is common for leaders and organizations to enter conversations with the aim of protecting their interests and defending their rights or their position. Calling this stage dialog is being generous, because this is entirely a one-way conversation, no matter how many parties are involved. Typical phrases include "You're wrong" and "Don't you understand what I am saying?"

   This does nothing to build trust or relationships, and may well harm them.

2. *Selling* It is just as common for conversations to revolve entirely around promoting an idea or a product. This sort of discussion is entirely about marketing; success here is defined in terms of whether one party got the other to do what it wanted. Typical phrases here include: "Let me tell you again why you should do this," or "Let me explain this to you again."

3. *Listening without hearing* By this stage, companies want to look like they are listening to what the other party says, but they have no plans to change anything because of it. The organization's spokesperson will probably say something like "What you have to say is very interesting," but he or she may well be thinking "Now let me tell you again why you should buy my product, or "When will this person stop talking so that I can make my point again."

4. *Listening, hearing, and reacting internally* This moves things on a step: after listening, the company incorporates ideas or insights from the discussion into what it does and how it does it. For example, a company might modify a product based on customer feedback, or change supply chain processes in response to complaints from environmental NGOs. The aim here is to improve what they do today based on genuine feedback.

5. *Co-creating* At this stage the emphasis moves from listening to a genuine conversation. The purpose of these dialogs is jointly to contribute to understanding issues and developing new solutions that benefit both parties. Here everyone involved works together to create and define new ways to build value in a manner that often extends beyond modifications to existing activities.

Moving up this dialog ladder requires moving from an attitude of defending entrenched positions to building mutual understanding. It also requires moving from an attitude of selling or promoting existing positions to defining new options and alternatives for the future. Finally it involves moving from an attitude of rigidity to one of flexibility, including looking at interactions as an important source of learning. All of these shifts are important building blocks for building the capacity to change and proactively respond, as opposed to holding onto the past.

From protecting independence to embracing interdependence The third element of the changing nature of interactions is driven by shifts in power and dependence between the parties. Reflect back on some of the changes highlighted in Rethinking Your Playing Field. We are seeing a growing dispersion of resources and knowledge, rising consumer demands, and changing societal expectations, among many others. In this world, there is a need for access and agility: access to the best resources and ideas, and agility in how they are integrated and employed.

Very few, if any, single company or institution owns or controls all of the resources and knowledge it needs, and cannot hope to do so in the future. This means that the need to interact and work with others will continue to grow. As a result, preparing for the future requires changes in the nature and mindset of company interactions and relationships with all stakeholders.

As described earlier, the transactional mindset involves all parties thinking and acting independently, with a focus on their own interests. But these transactional relationships are no longer sustainable. The days of independent control are giving way to a new world of interdependence and influence, through relationships. But putting collaboration into practice requires a major change in mindset, from "What do I independently own and control" to "Who are we working with, who can we influence, and how can we work together for our mutual benefit."

Success in the future will increasingly depend on working with an extended network of interdependent stakeholders, forging deeper relationships based on interdependence. As one CEO described it: "We are building relationships that result in enduring benefits not only for us, but also for those we interact with every day. If I do something where I win and you lose, you're not going to come back. Getting this right means creating a sustainable relationship where we both win."

Building relationships even extends to competitors

The idea of talking to competitors, let alone working with them, is likely to raise eyebrows, but it should not. It is possible to have a relationship with competitors without colluding, or engaging in anti-competitive behavior — both things that will damage trust and credibility, which is the exact opposite of what organizations need. We have observed a number of businesses who are doing this to achieve something much bigger than simply grabbing more market share. Instead, they are using such relationships to support their preparation for the future.

Positive competitor relationships are centered on acknowledgement that many of the challenges that the world faces will not be solved by governments or charities, but by businesses working in partnership with each other, and with organizations from other sectors.

Take pollution. Governments and regulators are doing what they can to create and enforce rules to reduce pollution, and related environmental and health damage, but they cannot do this fast enough. Often they are behind the pace of technological change, while the need to obtain agreement from a variety of individuals and organizations – even other governments – can slow things down even further.

Businesses could make a difference much faster if they were willing to work together. For example, we spoke to an executive at one company who told us that his firm had technology that would allow it to dramatically reduce pollution, but that it was not going to use it because it would place it at a disadvantage relative to its competitors.

This is an almost perfect illustration of the short-term trap in action. Companies that are preparing for the future recognize that it is in their long-term interests to reduce pollution: doing so will improve their reputation and their relationship with external stakeholders, not to mention protecting the resources on which all organizations in that market ultimately depend. Companies that are focused on immediate financial returns, by contrast, struggle to see past the up-front cost and the damage it will do to their profit margin.

But imagine what could be achieved if this company and its competitors had a relationship that allowed them to have a sensible conversation about pollution. They could define areas of co-operation and alignment; things that they agree on before they start competing. For example, if they all committed to using the same pollution-reducing technology, they could make a big difference to the environment without disadvantaging one business relative to another. Yes, they could wait until regulators decide to require all businesses to use this bit of technology, but that could take years.

We are starting to see this sort of conversation, often mediated by an industry body or similar forum, leading to self-regulation. For example, food companies are discussing how to protect critical natural resources and their environments, pre-competitively.

Or take the UK's Portman Group, which is backed by big-name drinks brands such as Diageo Great Britain, Carlsberg UK, AB InBev and Molson Coors UK, as an example. It was set up in 1989 by a group of alcohol businesses that wanted to promote sensible drinking and prevent alcohol misuse; several years later, it added encouraging sensible marketing and promotion to its remit. The industry also funds the Drinkaware alcohol education charity.

The question is how to extend and embrace these conversations and relationships across many more areas of global challenge, and many more businesses.

Perspectives from the front line: relationships

Harish Manwani *"You have to start first by recognizing that there is no premium on loyalty but there is a huge premium on commitment,"* Unilever's COO said of employees. *"When young people who join the company ask me, 'How long have you been in the company?' I say, 'I've worked here for more than 30 years, but I don't expect to get a medal just for being here that long.' The medal I would expect to get is for spending these years being committed.*

"So I say, 'My expectation from you, as young managers, is not your loyalty, but your commitment. When you are working with Unilever, are you 100% committed?'"

Anand Mahindra *"People are looking for meaning in their lives,"* Mahindra Group's chairman told us. *"The biggest malaise of the 21st century is a lack of meaning in people's lives.*

"You have to tell people to work toward a transcending goal, toward something more than achieving the next quarter's earnings. But as a CEO, you have to understand that you can't con people. You have to walk the talk and you have to smell honest. People know when you really believe in what you are saying. Fancy words alone will not keep people, but if you are true to yourself, you will start a movement. If you're even coming close to delivering this kind of value, believe me, you don't have to worry about how you will stay in front. You'll just get swept along with the tide."

Building relationships through dialog, alternatives, and flexibility: Port of Rotterdam

Incorporating dialog from the beginning was key to the way Hans Smits, the CEO of the Port of Rotterdam, managed a complex and highly controversial major expansion project involving multiple parties, many of which have a history of conflict.

"The issues we face are the challenges of developing and running the port," he told us. "About 90,000 people are involved in the port, from different organizations and with vastly different interests. We are more or less conducting this complex web of interactions. Because we influence our physical surroundings so much, we can only have the license to operate and grow if we have harmony with important stakeholders. After all, ports are highly visible as points of congestion and pollution, but also central to economic development.

"We also have to work at multiple levels. Globally we are directly involved in supporting and participating in global trade. For Europe we are part of the overall logistics infrastructure. For the Netherlands, we are an important source of employment and an attraction to industry. Locally we have a major role and impact on local industry and the local environment. Each layer requires taking a different perspective, looking at different information, thinking differently. We have to be able to adjust and accommodate all these different perspectives.

"One of our first reactions to this challenge was to bring into to our organization people who knew each of these interests intimately, so that we could anticipate and account for the differences. We brought in people from the chemical industry, from the logistics industry, from all of the other major industries that we interact with on a daily basis. We brought this insight inside our organization.

"One instance when our challenge is actually most complex is when we took on a major port expansion project, as this is when each party tries to protect their own interests. We are then also dealing with issues that not only affect today, but will have a major impact in the future. This makes our challenge very difficult. How can we develop a plan for the whole port that is acceptable to all of these different parties and reflects their different interests.

"Here we found our challenge is to discuss with all of the stakeholders, the national and international ones, about what we are going to do here. To accommodate all of these interests, we have to be flexible and to stay flexible. We can't rely on fixed master plans telling others what we are going to do. Rather we have to work with and involve all of these different parties from the start. We have to be flexible from the beginning, constantly thinking in alternatives to keep our options open.

"We have trained our people that if you get this city or environmental group against your plans, you do not start your discussions with what you want to do. Rather you start your talks by finding out what their interests are. This then becomes the basis of the dialog. This is a very important way to start discussions by talking about areas of interest, looking to understand and look for areas of common interest, as opposed to fighting over areas of difference.

"Here is where we have taken a very different but systematic approach and it has been very successful. We have found that in nine out of the 10 instances, if we truly understand both sides' issues we can almost always find solutions for potential conflicts. Because what we often found was that what you thought would be their problem was not the concern at all. They had other issues. And often you say, 'I can solve that immediately.' So our experience is mostly you come to a solution.

"Of course, in the end we did have to use the power play in some areas. There were two groups who in principle were against the project. We repeatedly tried to engage them in dialogs every year and they refused to come to the table. Finally we had to say 'fine, we see each other in court.' But overall what we found was that by taking this approach we have come up with solutions that were much better than our original plans."

Overall, Smits summarized the process he employs as follows: "Our strategy process is built around three phases: starting with dialog, thinking in alternatives, and then maintaining flexibility throughout the process. Doing this as an individual is hard, instilling it in an organization is even more difficult."

Ask yourself: are you moving from transactions to creative relationships?

The world of the future will be characterized by connections and interdependence, not traditional transactions. This means that you need to reshape how your organization interacts with all its stakeholders, internal and external.

Ask yourself:

Relationships Where are you organization's relationships with others on the transactional-collaborative scale? What about your own relationships as a leader?

Pressures What are the external – and internal – pressures encouraging more collaborative relationships? Are you really listening to them?

Conversations How can you build better dialogs?

Trust Given the pressure on immediate results, how can you give up control? How can you trust someone who does not report to you? How can you depend on someone outside your firm to do what you need to succeed, when it impacts your ability to meet your budgets and targets?

• •

Reshape what you do every day

The third topic in reshaping how you work involves changing what you do and how you do it, both inside and outside the organization.

Preparing for the future today is not about incremental maintenance of the status quo or reacting to change while constantly on the back foot. It is about visionary leadership that identifies the path ahead, and then takes on the even more difficult task of engaging the rest of the organization in traveling that path. This means challenging assumptions, finding new sources of advantage, and developing the new ways of working that will support it on its journey.

These new ways of working fall into three main areas: shifting from environments of complacency to ones of continual challenge; replacing old-style hierarchies with aligned, engaged employees; and relying on the power of values, trust, and commitment, rather than bureaucratic control.

From complacency to challenge

Organizational complacency comes in many shapes and forms. Most leaders will be familiar with people who insist that they are doing everything that they can given the limits of their job, or who promise that they have initiatives underway to address a particular issue, meaning that there is no need to give it further consideration − even if those initiatives are adding no real value. One clear indication of complacency is a pervading mindset of "We are a big successful company and will remain so."

What all forms of complacency share is an underlying preference for holding on to the past and sticking with the old ways of doing things. Tackling this issue requires leaders to build the courage, capacity, and commitment of individuals right across the organization so that they are all willing and able to challenge the status quo. Courage, in this scenario, is the understanding that stepping beyond traditional boundaries in every day work is accepted, and indeed expected. Capacity is having the tools and support needed to provide an effective challenge to traditional ways of working. Commitment is a passion to contribute to the long-term success of the organization, rather than simply concentrating on today's budgets.

Addressing complacency requires leaders to foster a workplace that provides the space for innovation and challenge, where people take ownership of the future direction of the firm. It's not about engaging in disruptive exchanges and internal battles and competition. Rather, the aim is to create an environment where employees are encouraged − expected, even − to constantly challenge the way the organization works in order to continually improve and strengthen its operations. There are a number of techniques that can support this.

Democratize information We live in a world of increasing transparency, but in many organizations information is power, and lack of information is lack of power, which can lead to information-hoarding behavior.

This, combined with today's complex organizational structures, means that the people who need information frequently do not get it, which in turn limits their ability to work, and to challenge complacency. Communication and information-sharing across the organization allows cross-pollination of ideas and improves innovation. An important challenge for leaders today is to democratize information, meaning that they must make information not a reflection of power, but view it as a tool to enable and support work. Leaders must ensure that information flows where it is needed.

Tap into the power of diversity Diversity is a critical factor when creating the capacity and capability to challenge. Whether it takes the shape of global cultural diversity, functional diversity – which minimizes the chance that one particular function dominates thinking – or gender diversity, the ability to tap into a wide variety of perspectives is extremely helpful.

Companies operating in complex markets will find that it is rare for one individual to have all of the insights and all of the answers. Diversity is needed to bring in different ideas and ways of thinking. We all learn more from people who are unlike us.

Achieving diversity is about much more than what Laura Liswood calls the Noah's Ark approach to hiring. "I think most organizations are stuck in the Noah's Ark period of diversity – let's just get two of each and we'll have our diversity," said Liswood, the author of The Loudest Duck and the secretary general of the Council of Women World Leaders. "It takes more than the metrics to realize the value of diversity," she told us. "There is a well-known, unfortunately anonymous, saying: 'We hire for difference and then we fire because they're not the same.' As long as there is a dominant power group, as long as there is no openness to listening, as long as there is no opportunity and ability to challenge ways of working, no firm will realize the potential of its diversity."

Another approach to diversity, and one which is particularly relevant given the growth markets of the future, involves not just bringing people in to headquarters, but moving people from headquarters into new regions. Executives who travel temporarily to different geographies will pick up more insights than those who merely observe from outside, but it is only by living in another country that they will develop a deep understanding of these markets by having "feet on the street" and regularly meeting local consumers. Without this understanding, their focus – and that of their organization – will always be that of the outsider thinking about what they can do in the market, rather than that of someone who understands how differences in these markets will fundamentally change and impact the future. Some companies are moving their top executives to offices in these regions to ensure that they understand the total environment and use this to set the organization's direction.

Engage the organization Many companies view strategy as the remit of senior management, with other employees playing a limited role in planning and budgeting. If extra insight or support is needed, they are more likely to call on external consultants than internal colleagues. This should change. Leaders should engage their whole organization to help them identify issues, not just to implement solutions.

Organizations that want their people to be truly engaged need to involve them in the whole strategy process. This requires leaders to find opportunities for employees to look outside the business, and the industry, to broaden their perspective. This will give them the chance to identify opportunities and bring insights back into the organization, to challenge the organization's traditional ways of working, and to help construct and even pilot solutions. It means tapping into the collective insights of all employees to define the future, rather than restricting them to maintaining current silos and ways of working.

Demand challenge Many organizations value constructive criticism and challenge – at least in theory. The tricky part is making sure that it is positively focused on moving the organization forward, rather than destructive, as can happen when things stray into territorial conflicts or the protection of partisan interests.

Leaders who want employees across the business to take ownership of the future direction of the firm need to reassure them that they have both the permission, and in fact the responsibility, to challenge how things work. This is not easy, as it demands new behaviors from both leaders and employees, and a high level of trust between them. For the leader, it requires humility, and the confidence to see challenge not as a threat to personal power, but as a vehicle for addressing issues. For employees, it requires stepping out of the comfortable "I just do what I am told" mindset and taking responsibility for identifying and addressing issues and opportunities.

From hierarchical control to employee empowerment

Empowerment is likely one of the most overused and under-practiced concepts in business today. All that talk hides the reality that often executives are unwilling to give up any control, instead demanding detailed information and involvement in many decisions – the opposite of empowerment. The traditional belief that top managers are the organization's primary decision-makers is a hard habit to break.

At the other extreme is the view that the leadership team's role is to shape and continually update the direction of the firm, to define and own the framework within which the organization operates, to hire and challenge the best, motivated employees – and then to step out of the way and let them get on with it.

Paul Bulcke, the CEO of Nestlé, illustrated the difference with a military analogy. "In peacetime, a soldier thinks about the sergeant, who thinks about the captain, and so on. It is all inward and upward looking. This is much like we find in many organizations today. However, in the first hour of war this orientation turns 180 degrees. Everybody thinks about the soldier, because who else is going to win the war? Soldiers are going to be the people who make the difference. They have to have the best shoes, the best equipment, the best strategy, the best inspiration, and the best motivation. It is the same in business, where we have to battle every day."

There are a number of steps that can help to place a business on a permanent war footing:

Look beyond job descriptions Tight, formal job descriptions divide an organization into small pieces focused on traditional activities. They promote internal power struggles, rather than encouraging people to work together to identify opportunities. They can trap organizations into perpetuating past ways of working and thinking, and discourage them from looking outside their own walls. When people are engaged, they don't need pieces of paper to define their activities and roles; instead, this is shaped by the ever-changing markets in which they operate.

Instill freedom within a framework Businesses need to put empowerment into practice. This means turning their organizations upside down and recognizing that daily decisions made at the front line are critical to business success. Breaking the traditional top-down processes involves making space for innovation, where people are aligned and take ownership of the direction of the firm.

Removing old constraints does not mean that the workplace will descend into anarchy. Leaders need to build and communicate a clear framework that will provide enough guidance to allow people to take independent action, while still moving the organization in a consistent direction. That is, the organization sets direction and context, and trusts individuals to use their initiative to be as innovative and creative as they like within this.

This framework should incorporate many of the elements we describe in this book: a view of the future business environment and your firm's desired position within it (Rethink Your Playing Field); the company's purpose, vision, and metrics, which provide the overall path to the future (Redefine Your Ambition); and the company's expectations about how it, and its employees, interact with other stakeholders.

It must also be communicated clearly and consistently across the whole organization. The message should be: "This is what our future could look like.

This is who we are. This is where we are going. This is what we expect of you." The result should be alignment and engagement across the firm.

The other important tool here is a cascade process that allows leaders and employees to explore the implications of the overall agenda for different parts of the business. The most effective approach is usually to start with the big picture before focusing in on the implications, opportunities, and challenges for each specific part of the business. It's a similar process to the steps outlined in this book: start by building insights into what is happening, then explore what it means for your part of the organization, and finally identify the actions you need to take both to deliver today and prepare for the future.

Freedom within a framework: Gucci

"We do manage our brands. But you don't manage people, you lead them and you coach them," Robert Polet, the former CEO of Gucci Group, told us. "This involves creating an environment in which creativity is allowed to flourish. Creativity is not managed, it emerges."

Creating the right environment for creativity to flourish means hiring the right people, but, more than that, it means giving them freedom within a clear set of parameters, he said.

"If you have defined the brand position and told the top team 'This is what you want to achieve over time and this is what you need to achieve each year,' you then trust these people to get on with it," he said. For example, Polet was never involved in product design, and very rarely gave a judgment even when asked, because that is his creative director's job. "A designer creates products that you and I are not yet aware of, and it's only when we see them that we think 'That's what I desire, that's what I need'," he said.

"So our head designer works within the context of the positioning of the Gucci brand, and within a brief from the merchandising department. They make a grid of all the bags that are the competition, then say 'We want a bag in this space here for 1,500 with those sort of functionalities. We also want an appropriate gross margin. Now be creative and create me a bag.' And after that there's no other involvement. After that, she decides."

The head designer also has complete autonomy over how she runs her team of 70 designers: Polet did not watch over how she or other leaders managed their operations, although he did provide support in the form of coaching, when needed.

"The senior management team does not take over difficult decisions, but instead encourages our leaders to take their own difficult decisions," he said. "I always said 'Look, we hold hands, okay? You take the decision, but I'm holding hands with you. When there's a success, you did it, but when it's failure, we did it.'"

Operating like this takes more energy, but it is the only way to get the best out of people, he said.

From bureaucracy to the power of values, trust and commitment

Insistence upon strict, hierarchical control is one of the clearest signs that an organization is clinging on to the old ways of doing things. Organizations that think in bureaucratic boxes also tend to have a real problem with fragmentation: each business unit thinks, and acts, as if it were its own fiefdom. There is no sense that each part is working towards the same goal, let alone effective knowledge-sharing between them. Headquarters exists to ensure compliance rather than to promote cooperation and collaboration, or to support and enable success.

Such companies struggle to take the outside-in look at the world needed to rethink their playing field or redefine their ambition. Their need for control and intense internal focus also slows them down, making them reactive to external events rather than getting ahead of change.

The thought of giving up control makes many managers extremely uncomfortable, but, as long as people are aligned behind a clear, shared vision, this is the only way to tap into what other people have to offer an organization. It does not mean that the need for central staff is eliminated, but that their primary function shifts from control to supporting and enabling both top leadership and organizational units.

The struggle to significantly reduce unnecessary bureaucracy is not new, and is a critical part of reshaping how people work: not by relying on new rulebooks and stricter controls, but by embedding purpose-driven values into the business, and then allowing people to find their own paths to the organization's goals. This builds on the establishment of entrepreneurial empowerment and freedom within a framework.

Making this attitude meaningful means moving beyond the "words on a wall" approach to one in which values are embedded in a daily experience that depends on trust and true empowerment, and is paired with real accountability. Such trust allows an organization to tap into the passion, energy, and commitment of its employees.

As the roles of and relationships with employees change, leaders need to devote even more effort to people and the selection of leaders within the firm.

Focus on relationships, not roles Most large organizations, and their employees, operate in a complex matrix. This is because optimizing a business along a single dimension of its activities – whether products, geographies, or functions – to the exclusion of others does not fully address today's and tomorrow's challenges and opportunities. This is why most executives and leaders have multiple responsibilities.

The problem comes when an executive focuses on one role at the expense of his or her other responsibilities, or ignores their larger potential contribution to the organization. When this happens, silo thinking emerges. Such divisions don't fit well with a world that requires choices and trade-offs, and can mean that the success of the business as a whole is subordinated to silo-based interests.

One explanation for this dysfunctional behavior is that putting individuals in boxes or roles often results in internal political posturing. The solution is to shift the focus of the organization from a "this is my job" mindset to one in which everyone prioritizes the success of the business as a whole. Broadening the focus and responsibility of leaders – in fact, all employees – in this way means that one person or division cannot deliver on the firm's opportunities and challenges alone. It will require working together and building strong cross-functional and cross-organizational relationships to address them.

Show your people that they matter Trust is a two-way street, but many organizations have lost the trust of their key employees. One executive told us about a recent experience that highlighted this perfectly. "I hadn't seen this guy for two weeks, and I said 'Sorry I did not have enough time to get back to you.' He said, 'You're kidding me. You have time. You have 24 hours a day, but I just wasn't your priority.' And that was a lesson learned."

The message, which we heard over and over again, is that actions speak louder than words. Senior leaders need to demonstrate every day that they care about the organization, about its people and what they stand for. Even if short of time, what you don't do sends as loud a message as what you do.

The late Morris Tabaksblat, the former CEO of Unilever and chairman of Reed Elsevier, offered an explanation of why this decline in trust has happened. "The core of the relationship is a two-way commitment that is not based on the concept of a job, but on a mutual belief in something," he told us. "This relationship is challenged in many firms by endless rounds of restructuring because people say, 'I am here to serve and I have to do this tough job and get rid of so many people, but am I next?' You can do this for a period because people see the logic and understand why it happened. But you can't keep doing it because it leads to cynicism and a loss of commitment. The employee is not at fault here, the company is at fault for allowing this situation to arise."

Organizations must move beyond paying lip service to the idea that their people are their most important assets. Actions – including the things leaders choose not to do, as well as those they do – speak louder than words. It is up to senior leaders to demonstrate every day that they care about the organization, about its people, and about what they stand for.

Instill values and trust as the foundations for behavior Values can become the organization's behavioral guidelines, the glue that holds everything together. Think of a company's agenda as the framework that shows people what they should be doing, and its values as the framework that tells them how they should be doing it. The roots of many company crises can be traced to people concentrating too much on what they are trying to achieve, and not enough on how they are trying to achieve it.

This is not the same as rigid rules about what is and is not allowed. Such an approach is bound to leave gaps, and is virtually begging people to look for loopholes. The better analogy is that a values framework gives people a moral compass, and then trusts them to judge what is right in any given situation. Freeing people up from bureaucracy and trusting them contribute to real empowerment.

Values can also be used to support business discipline. Mahindra Group, which we discussed earlier, is guided both by its purpose, and by a strong set of values that shape behaviors. In addition, it has a disciplined approach to business that is embodied in mantras that outline specific performance expectations, along with rigorous measurements and KPIs for each. Values and discipline are both necessary, but neither alone is enough for success.

Together they create a powerful engine to drive behaviors and activities, engaging and guiding individuals while providing them with the room needed to drive the company forward.

Apply values consistently, internally and externally Values have to mean something if they are to make any real difference; they have to be more than a slogan. Part of that means that organizations, and their leaders, need to apply those values consistently to all relationships, both internal and external. At its extreme, this principle could mean that an otherwise positive business partnership needs to be rejected because an organization and its potential partner do not share common values. This is partly because values act as glue in external relationships, just as they do internally, and partly because, in this networked world, organizations will be judged by the company they keep. Organizations that claim one set of values for themselves but do not expect them of suppliers, for example, will be damaged.

Burn the operating manual!

Harish Manwani of Unilever took dramatic steps to break his senior team out of a traditional, bureaucratic way of thinking. "When I ran Latin America, Unilever was moving from a country to a regional structure," he told us. "It was the right thing to do, but people were getting obsessed internally with who would do what in the new operating framework. At one of my first leadership events, in which the top 100 Latin American leaders participated, I asked them to bring their operating manuals. Throughout the day, we discussed a common set of goals and our definition of business success.

"At the end of that day, we gathered in an open area to watch the sunset. Everyone was given a lighter, and just as the sun set I said, 'Now, put a torch to the operating framework. From here on, no one is going to consult the framework.

"That is the point at which we moved from roles to relationships. You cannot run an organization through manuals. If you've got a problem, you pick up the phone and talk to the right person. The glue is always common goals and values."

• •

Perspectives from the front line: new ways of working

Peter Brabeck-Letmathe Some of Nestlé's regional CEOs used to delay sharing information from group headquarters with their local leadership teams, the company's chairman told us. *"Every single person in the pyramid was using information as a power tool,"* he said.

His response, as group CEO, was to democratize information. *"We make sure that the same information is available to all of our employees, not just the ones attending meetings. In the past, information was power – not any more. Many leadership conferences are now broadcast online so that anyone within the company with a computer can see what is discussed, while other information is shared in writing and online. You don't have to wait for anybody anymore. Everybody has the same access to information."*

Ben Vree *"I see a job description as limitation,"* the former CEO of Smit International told us. *"If you let it define your role, then you suggest that you must have this little document so you can say, 'I'm your boss. See, here it is mentioned.' Well, that is not the right mentality. I often tell those people, when you run too fast, by the time that you step on somebody else's toes, you will know soon enough what your role could be."*

Bengt Braun *"When I became CEO I started out by defining the basic values of the company,"* said Braun, who is now vice-chairman of Bonnier Group. *"What do we particularly value in our people and what do we demand from our managers? And what type of work environment should we have?*

"The ideal is one of trust. Trust allows people to be their best. If you want to develop and allow your people to stick their necks out, you must give them the space to do so."

Marcelo Odebrecht *"Some people find it difficult to believe that I know more or less a couple of thousand people in the company,"* the CEO of Odebrecht, told us. *"But most of my time is really dedicated to this. It is not only a question of establishing long-term trust and commitment, it is also critical because when you make a key appointment you have to find people that can complement each other. It's not just a question of identifying and putting the right person in the right place; you must help to make the whole team complementary."*

• •

Ask yourself: have you reshaped how you work?

Rethinking and redefining are important exercises – indeed, they are critically important – but on their own they are not enough to bring about real change. For that to happen, you and your organization need to change what you do every day, and how you do it.

Ask yourself:

Framework Does your organization have a clear framework, within which you can empower people to give the best they can to move the company forward?

Information Do you provide people with the information they need to be entrepreneurial and to think about what matters to the company as a whole, not just their part of it?

Values Do you use values to guide behavior and actions? Are these values understood the same way across the firm? Do you apply them consistently, internally and externally?

Trust Have you built mutual trust and commitment between yourself, your leadership team, and your people? Do you know what behaviors and attitudes you, and the team as a whole, still need to change?

Approach Are you supporting the changes you want to make? For example, are you tapping into the power of diversity? Are you promoting a culture of courage and challenge?

• •

Challenging boards: from mercenaries to missionaries

We've written this book for all leaders who hold significant roles within their organizations, not just group CEOs and presidents. We do not assume that all of our readers will have direct experience of working with boards of directors. However, we hope that those who do will find this next section useful and challenging.

Financial markets are a big driver of short-term thinking, largely because of the emphasis they place on maximizing immediate shareholder returns. CEOs who want to prepare their organizations for the future have started asking questions about who these shareholders are, what impact they are having on the business, and whether there is anything they can do about it.

The short answer is yes: CEOs are beginning to focus on influencing their company's ownership. They are beginning to encourage shareholders who want long-term sustainable growth, rather than profits made through short-term trading. And they are beginning to work with the owners' representatives, the board of directors, to ensure that the board itself is not swayed by the whims of short-term traders and analysts.

Equally, it is up to directors to take responsibility for ensuring the CEO leads in a way that is aligned with the company's long-term interests. For too long board directors have been happy to let CEOs lead companies in the interests of short-term shareholders. However, if CEOs and boards wish their businesses to succeed in the future, they must rebalance this relationship. They need to work together so that activities and decision-making are focused on long-term success, not just short-term survival.

The role of boards here is central because they are ultimately responsible to the company's owners – its shareholders – not to the company's management. This responsibility raises a number of important questions: What is the relationship between company management and the board, and how does this shape the agenda and focus of the company? To which shareholders are boards accountable, and how do they reflect this accountability in their ongoing activities? How do boards define, and ultimately represent, owner interests through their relationship with a business's CEO and senior management team?

How we got to where we are today: mercenary boards

In the early days the typical board was little more than an old boys' club: the CEO invited his contacts and friends, typically people with a very similar outlook to his own, to join the board. In return, they were generally happy enough to let him (or very occasionally her) get on with things. The role of the board at this point was less to protect the interests of shareholders than to protect the interests of the CEO; the idea of a director challenging the CEO about his or her decisions was almost unthinkable.

Things started to change when businesses were hit by a series of highly-visible scandals, from Enron to Parmalat. This resulted in growing shareholder activism and significant regulatory changes that made corporate governance more rigorous, financial practices more transparent, and management more accountable. This was, and continues to be, a good and necessary thing. In parallel with this, analysts and activist shareholders increased their scrutiny of the financial performance of firms, including emphasizing short-term, often quarterly reporting.

However, one outcome of this greater attention to detail is that many boards have become more like an internal audit or risk function than a leadership group. It has created a class of people who are professional board members, often sitting on multiple boards. Actions related to financial reporting, risk management, reforms, and executive compensation are heavily scrutinized by shareholders, regulators, and governance rating agencies. Boards are being called on to devote their time to verifying and ensuring immediate compliance at the expense of other activities representing shareholder interests.

One director told us: "Today you have to sign off on many areas where you don't know in detail, or with certainty, what you are signing. Not only does this not feel responsible, it also makes one really uncomfortable. For many of our decisions, we don't get to do due diligence, but we still have to decide what our assessment is. When decisions go wrong, we often hear people say 'The board was asleep.' They weren't. They were probably working very hard. But the board is dependent on the perspectives and the data that's presented to it." However, this mercenary compliance and approval focus continues and, as a result of new regulatory requirements, the threat of penalties, and a stronger emphasis on enforcement, directors are at increasing risk of personal civil and criminal liability.

So in the all-important relationship between boards and CEOs, most boards are time-constrained, under-informed, and under-involved; their main focus is approving budgets and proposals put forward by company management, and ensuring regulatory compliance. CEOs themselves face increasing pressure from analysts and markets, and the board members, who are the representatives of shareholders, simply follow along. In these conditions, driving long-term, sustainable growth simply does not get attention.

As one CEO mentioned: "We've given a lot of power to bankers and financiers. We've given them a high degree of control of the corporate agenda. But the whole concept of shareholder value is not what these analysts and their static models project." As we pointed our earlier, another added: "Members of the financial community used to recognize their role as being the oil that lubricates and enables the economic engine. Too often today they view themselves as the engine itself." The danger of ceding the corporate agenda to financiers' control is a challenge for business leaders and their boards.

What businesses need from boards today is not an ever-increasing focus on approvals and compliance, or passive agreement to short-term strategies, but recognition that they are shareholders' representatives. Organizations need boards and directors with the time, energy, and ability to focus on the specifics of the business and what it will take for it to succeed in the future. They also need boards with a willingness to stand up for the company's long-term interests against market pressures that push for the short term.

Unfortunately, too often what they get is people who read the papers on the way to their next board meeting and who know little more about the business than whether or not its numbers add up. It is hardly surprising that they give the CEO such a free hand.

Where we need to be: missionary boards

Businesses do not need mercenary boards filled with people who can read balance sheets or assess risk registers; they can – and indeed, already do – appoint professional auditors to do those things. What they need is a missionary board: a group of people with a deep understanding of the business, relevant experience, and willingness to challenge and influence the CEO in the name of owners who have an interest in the long-term, sustainable success of the business. They need to be evangelists – missionaries – who want to lead the business towards the right path.

Companies need to be prepared to prioritize the interests of long-term shareholders over short-term traders. Theoretically, board directors are there to represent the interests of all shareholders. However, there are clear differences in the interests and focus of different types of shareholders. Some invest in companies solely on the basis of the potential for immediate returns from price volatility, irrespective of whether this volatility is upward or downward. These short-term owners have no interest in the future success, or even survival, of the company. By contrast, longer-term shareholders have a greater interest in the longer-term success of a business.

We believe that that managers, and boards, owe their primary responsibility to those with a longer-term interest in a business. Traders do not value businesses for what they create or what they contribute. They view them simply as commodities, as they would any other trading instrument. They are not interested in the fact that only businesses can create real value; they only care about what they can offer when playing the markets.

Prioritizing long-term shareholders requires boards to help move the company from having a mission statement on the wall to being purpose-led, and from having a vision, which is often little more than a marketing slogan, to being truly vision-led. This means moving beyond a dominant focus on today's markets, competitors, customers, and capabilities to develop a perspective on how future trends are reshaping the world. Company leadership, including the missionary board, should define the direction in which firms must evolve to prepare for this future. Being a purpose led organization emphasizes creating the internal alignment, focus, and guidelines that shape the direction of company activities.

For a missionary board, purpose and vision become fundamental building blocks in supervising and working with the CEO and senior company leadership to set the future direction and agenda of a business. While ensuring short-term performance and regulatory compliance remain important board tasks, a strong focus on ensuring long-term success, which requires more direct involvement of the board, must move to the fore.

Mercenary versus missionary boards

	Mercenary boards [Bureaucratic compliance committees]	Missionary boards [Representatives of long-term stakeholders]
Board role	• Formal approvals • Ensuring regulatory compliance • Risk mitigation	• Supervising short-term operations • Ensuring organizational preparedness for sustainable success • Shaping and protecting institutional vision and purpose
Composition	• Prestige directors • Specialist directors	• Diverse, committed individuals with strategic and institutional insight
Way of working	• Individuals • Focused committees	• As a team committed to the sustainable success of the organization
Relationship with CEO & management	• CEO plays strong part in determining the board's role • Mixed levels of transparency and challenge	• Transparent and trusting
Chairman's role	• Manage board processes • Oversee committee activities	• Responsible for successful functioning of the board
Focus	• Ongoing compliance • Short-term financial performance	• Long-term sustainability of the organization

Making the change

Creating missionary boards, and persuading CEOs to engage with and listen to them, will take both time and some fundamental changes in the composition, role, and behavior of the board. Technically and legally, CEOs report to the board, but on a practical level many treat it as little more than a formal approval process. One CEO we interviewed said: "If the board starts to interfere in the day-to-day process, it's fatal. If they think they have to, they should just get rid of the CEO."

A director, on the other hand, told us that boards want CEOs to ask their opinion. He said: "Many boards want very much to contribute to the company; they want to be involved and listened to. Many directors are looking for the CEO to say 'What do you think? How should we do this?' When that dynamic exists, it can be pretty powerful. But the CEO has to want to do it. Some CEOs are good listeners, but many aren't. And if they aren't good listeners, then there's no sense talking."

While the sentiment expressed by the CEO suggests a certain degree of arrogance, it is impossible not to sympathize with his concerns. After all, a director's input will only be useful to the CEO if he or she has a deep understanding of the company – which is why organizations need to do much more to ensure that board members are able fully to understand the business of the company they serve. It is only under these circumstances that boards can provide valuable strategic input for their organization.

The who as well as the what

Moving from a mercenary to a missionary board is not simply about the role of the board or the issues on which it focuses; it is also about its composition – the directors who, individually and collectively, facilitate the transformation. Creating a missionary board means finding new types of directors and establishing new ways of working within the board, and, most importantly, with the company's CEO and senior executive leadership.

Making these changes will not be easy. Altering the board's way of working and its relationship with the CEO is probably one of the most significant challenges in the transition from mercenary to missionary boards. It will involve building transparency and trust – two characteristics often missing in today's mercenary boards. Only then will there be an effective forum for exploring options and challenging the thinking and perspectives of company leadership. And only then will the board be able to make a strong contribution to supervising and shaping the long-term vision and purpose that will ultimately establish and shape the agenda, activities, and direction of the business.

Building a missionary board requires change on both sides, but the starting point has to be trust. "Trust is absolutely crucial," one former CEO, now the director of several large companies, told us. "You can have the best short-term plans, but if the guys who are governing the institution do not have full trust in the plan and what is behind it, things start to go wrong. Today many CEOs view boards simply as places to get approval. But the relationship between a CEO and a board has so much more potential."

While boards typically do not, and should not, get involved in the actual operation of the business, directors' ability to do their jobs is highly dependent on their relationship with the CEO and company leadership. Evidence from our research suggests that many CEOs already struggle to take directors' views into account. One highly-experienced director told us: "The CEOs that really consult members of a non-executive board, tapping into their skills and experience, are very rare. It is very difficult for a CEO to go to a board and say 'This is what I'm thinking. What do you think?' Also, directors may not be active enough to really understand what is going on in a company. Most are not drawn to be on the board to really engage with management; they are motivated by some other reasons."

Just as directors need to take more time to engage with the company, CEOs need to open up about what they are thinking and why they are thinking it. Openness on both sides helps to create a board that allows much more robust debate and in turn delivers stronger, more thoughtful strategic guidance. "The best boards are transparent boards," one director told us. "I work with one CEO who is the most transparent that I've ever seen. He lays all the cards on the table. It seems there's nothing he's afraid to tell us and ask our opinion about. Likewise, the best boards are the boards that have people who will express their opinion rather than just go along with everyone else when they don't really agree with something."

The independent chairman's role

The chairman plays a major role in how the board works and whether it operates on a mercenary or a missionary model. It is the chairman's job to shape relations with the leadership of the company, structure the tasks and focus of the board, guide the selection of board members, and create the environment in which the board works. The chairman is also responsible for working with, coaching, and supervising the CEO.

Combining the role of chairman with that of CEO, as is still common in a number of U.S.-based companies, is questionable for all these reasons. It is only with an independent chairman that a missionary board will have the strength and focus needed to represent the interests of its long-term shareholders, and to provide both support and challenge to management.

And it is only with the leadership and guidance of an independent chairman that missionary boards are created. "First of all, the chairman has to change," one director told us. "They have to want to be the conscience of the company and the supreme court of the company. This raises the important issue of who chooses the chairman of the board. As long as it's a CEO who wants to keep running the show, this change in the role of the board won't be enabled."

The demands on the chairman of a missionary board are significant even when the transformation to the new model is complete. Some of the executives we interviewed went so far as to suggest that the chairman has a special responsibility for a firm's long-term performance. "The board chairman needs to look out for the really long term," one executive told us. "It cannot be the CEO, because the CEO is too busy and will always be measured and benchmarked against current markets and competitors. A CEO cannot afford to really differ much from the market's expectations."

The chairman needs to find a balance between supporting the CEO and ensuring that major topics are put on the board's agenda. This involves a serious time commitment; several interviewees said that being an effective chairman can mean working up to three days per week in the company.

Taking on the challenge

Gone are the days of prestige appointments, when a director served on 10 or more boards. Gone are the days when a director's involvement was limited to attending formal meetings. Business has entered the era of the missionary board, for all that we are still in its very early days. Organizations are now starting to realize they must identify and attract long-term owners if they are to build sustainable success. They are beginning to understand that their boards must have a clear view of their purpose, and a commitment representing the interests of those long-term owners.

But the evolution to a missionary model is not, as we have seen, a simple change. It is one that requires both CEOs and directors to think, act, and work differently. It requires entrenched attitudes and relationships to be shaken up, or even replaced entirely. It would be easy for a business leader to look at such changes and decide they are too unsettling, too demanding, to be worth the effort. It would be easy, in the short term at least, to continue with business as usual.

Such a decision would, however, condemn that leader's organization to an inevitable decline. The only realistic option for companies competing in today's increasingly volatile, uncertain world is to prepare for the long term. Focus on short-term success will simply not stand up to the pressure of the radical changes happening in the world looking forward.

Reshape how you work: recap

Build your agenda: balance sprints and marathons Budgets, plans, and strategies are frequently misunderstood or misused by executives who think that they are working strategically when they are actually using a budget or a plan, both of which are more short-term oriented tools. Strategy should be developed first, as it guides the company's long-term direction. Plans and budgets can then be built to support this strategy.

Two-directional thinking comes in to this process as a way for leaders to identify which short-term, low-priority issues are taking up time today, and should be resolved fast (sprints), and which long-term actions must be sustained (marathons) to ensure the organization is prepared for the future.

Move from transactions to creative relationships Businesses are used to transactional relationships, which are defined by buying and selling, but relationships of the future will be much more complex, subtle, and long-lasting than these one-off arrangements. The power balance between business and consumers, employees, and other stakeholders has shifted along with their expectations; organizations and their leaders must reshape the way they interact with these groups to build relationships based on collaboration and mutual value creation.

Reshape what you do every day The early part of this book has focused on how leaders need to change the way they think in order to bridge the gap between short-term profit and long-term sustainable success, but a changed mindset is not enough: organizations need to reshape what they do every day. They need to encourage employees to challenge the status quo; replace old-fashioned hierarchies with independent employees who are free to work as they see fit, within a clear framework; and use the power of shared values, not bureaucracy, to guide people's actions.

Challenging boards: from mercenaries to missionaries CEOs who want to prepare their organizations for the future need to think differently about who their shareholders are if they want to escape the short-term trap. Shareholders – and their representatives, the board of directors – can play a critical role in shaping and supporting preparations for long-term business sustainability, but achieving this means that CEOs and boards need to reshape how they work together.

As a leader you must address six key challenges to reshape how you work:

1. Identify where you need to address immediate issues to strengthen your business today. Develop an accelerated action plan for these sprints.

2. Identify where you need to fundamentally transform your business. Develop a long-term action plan that will sustain progress throughout these marathons.

3. Translate your ambition into a long-term strategy, and then use that as the foundation for planning and budgeting. Do not allow budgets and other short-term plans to define the agenda.

4. Redefine short-term transactional relationships to build committed, long-term relationships with all key stakeholders – consumers, employees, suppliers, society, and owners.

5. Address organizational complacency by building the courage, capacity, and commitment needed to challenge current ways of working and thinking.

6. Shift the leadership focus from top-down decision making to creating the environment for engaging, aligning and empowering employees across the organization.

None of the changes that we have described in this chapter or the two preceding it are simple. They require a fundamental change in how leaders approach their organization's market, its purpose, its stakeholders, and its operations. But it is not just how they change in relation to the world around them that matters; ultimately, leaders need to change themselves as individuals if they, too, are to be prepared for the future. In the next chapter, we look at how leaders should apply the 3Rs of preparing for success to their own personal and professional development.

Measure your progress

Use the following table to assess where you are today in terms of reshaping how you work. Remember, key ideas introduced in this chapter are in the shaded rows of text, while column 1 describes the least advanced and 5 describes the most advanced state of practice in companies today. Options 2 or 4 mean your company is somewhere in between each state of practice.

As before, go through this assessment twice: once from your organization's perspective, and once from your own personal position. Have others in your senior leadership team – as well as people lower down the organization, and even your broader stakeholders – complete the exercise independently to gain additional insights.

1	2	3	4	5
Balance sprints and marathons				
Our agenda is driven by short-term initiatives to strengthen us today and react to short-term opportunities and challenges; many have been going on for some time		We have some initiatives to prepare us for long-term success, but the majority of our agenda is built around the short term; we are accelerating addressing issues which hold us back		Our agenda has a balanced mix of sprints and marathons
Use of budgets, plans and strategies				
Budgets rule, although we do some planning for the medium term		We use all three, but not necessarily in the right order; our planning cycle is well established		The use of all three tools is well established; strategy drives plans and then budgets
Approach to relationships				
We are a sales machine; you have to push hard all the time to drive success and loyalty to increase sales		We balance push and pull approaches; we build strong, interactive relationships with our customers, employees, and stakeholders		Our relationships reflect interdependence and mutual interests, allowing us to co-create solutions that create new value; commitment is critical
Challenging current thinking and ways of working				
We are a big, successful company and will remain so – everyone knows that		We value diverse opinions; people are encouraged to challenge how we do things, but sometimes this can be disruptive		Our workplace and leadership commitment foster real innovation and challenge – people take ownership of creating the future

1	2	3	4	5
Approach to employee empowerment				
We have clear structures, processes, and job descriptions; leaders make decisions and provide people with targets against which they can execute and be measured		Our people understand the direction and ambition of the company and their role within this; they have the space to contribute if they choose		We have freedom within a framework and a clear ambition; leaders develop and communicate the framework consistently, so everyone can contribute according to their potential
Approach to values, trust, and commitment				
Our values are just words on a wall; tasks and targets are subject to strict control by headquarters		We have a climate of collaboration, with relationships based on trust and understanding of our values, but KPIs are still important		Our values drive behaviors and relationships, internally and externally; mutual trust and commitment is our organizational glue

FIVE: The 3Rs of Preparing Yourself for the Future

Preparing an organization for the future, while delivering immediate results, is one of the biggest, most important, and most difficult leadership tasks that any executive will undertake. It is a challenge that requires leaders to manage numerous simultaneous changes to ensure that they reshape their business for long-term success without losing sight of short-term needs. Rethinking the playing field, redefining the organization's ambition, and reshaping how it works every day need to become an almost instinctive part of the approach to business; effectively, the 3Rs form the basis of a new attitude to what companies do, why they do it, and how they do it.

However, there is one final, critical element that leaders need to change in parallel to all this: their own individual attitude to leadership and to their own lives. If their approach to leadership is stuck in the past, they will struggle to provide the leadership that their organization will need in the future. Old ways of thinking about and approaching leadership are just as damaging to organizations as old ways of thinking about competition or of operating a business. In our interviews we have seen some apparently self-interested, short-term leaders holding organizations back, just as we have also seen leaders who have created a powerful force for change by combining future-ready attitudes to business and to leadership.

Unless leaders are prepared to reexamine how they live their personal lives and how they prepare for their roles as leaders and individuals, they may become exhausted and lose touch with what is takes to succeed. Organizational success cannot happen without the personal success of the leader, and the success of those working with or living with him or her. Just as the world is becoming interdependent, so too are our lives, work, and the communities with which we interact.

Preparing yourself for the future

Why do executives need to develop a different attitude to leadership and life? For much the same reason that they need to rethink, redefine, and reshape their approach to business. That is, the world is changing, and the demands of leaders are changing with it. The men and women who sit at the top of organizational structures now and in the future will need different skills and abilities to those who have led companies – albeit successfully – in the past.

They are dealing with new levels of complexity, uncertainty, and volatility. Unless they are open to change, and prepared to get ahead of it, they will hold back their organizations, not lead them.

For example, obviously hierarchical power is waning. In years gone by, leaders could rely on the authority of their position to command enough respect to get things done; employees were used to being told what to do. Today, as organizations move towards freedom within a framework and other less-bureaucratic approaches to get the most from their people, a command and control style will no longer be effective, even though many leaders still cling to it: leaders need to find a new way to lead.

Similarly, the emergence of connections, not boxes, as the defining characteristic of business today means that leaders need to think afresh about how they build the necessary relationships, inside and outside their organizations.

These connections extend beyond a leader's role at work to his or her role in life. Leaders cannot truly be successful if they are exhausted and isolated outside work. Leadership and life are becoming increasingly complex and intertwined. In fact, many leaders spoke about work-life issues not in terms of balance, but of integration. Personal life informs and enables work life, with the reverse being equally true.

In this chapter we look at how leaders can use the 3Rs model to examine and change their own approach to life and leadership at the same time as they change their organization in readiness for the future. We encourage leaders to rethink what it means to be a successful leader and a successful individual, and what is required to fulfill those roles; to redefine their purpose, values, and principles; and to reshape how they lead, how they live, and how they connect.

This is a process that requires time, effort, and courage. It is not easy, and in some cases it may force individuals to confront difficult decisions, but in the end leaders will find that being able to align their purpose with that of the organization will benefit them, their organization, and the world more broadly.

One final note: our collective experience suggests that the most powerful change processes are those that recognize the intricate linkages between personal leadership development, leadership team development, and building organizational readiness for the future. It is very easy to send senior executives off to feel good about themselves and/or their teams when they do not have to confront real challenges. It is equally easy to sit managers down to discuss strategy when everyone knows that they will not have to make any personal changes.

What is much more difficult, but infinitely more effective, is to combine the two. So, when we are working with leadership teams we often spend the days talking about the changes that the organization needs to make, and the evenings discussing what it means for individuals within the team and their own personal development. Putting both these things together to form one coherent whole results in a much more powerful, aligned approach, and one which should mean that both individuals and their organization develop together in parallel.

Provincials and pioneers: where are leaders today?

The first part of this book highlighted the split between companies that are holding onto the past, and those that are investing in owning the future. One of the clearest and most important differentiating factors between such organizations was their leader and his or her personal attitude towards what was to come, and how businesses should prepare. Here we found two distinct approaches among leaders: provincials, who want stick to the old ways and wish the rest of the world would too; and pioneers, who are excited about the changes ahead, and want to play a part in shaping them, as well as preparing for them. In many cases leaders exhibit characteristics from each end of the spectrum, although most tend to be closer to one end than the other.

How leaders are coping with the pressures for change

Holding onto the past		Focused on owning the future
Overwhelmed: with the pace and extent of change		**Informed**: about the array of broad changes shaping the future
Oblivious: to the bigger picture of the changes underway		**Insightful**: about the implications of the changes on their organization
Opportunistic: looking at changes only through the lens of meeting short-term targets		**Inspirational**: in guiding the organization to prepare for the future

Provincials At one extreme we see leaders who are overwhelmed by the challenges they face. They struggle to make sense of the myriad changes taking place in the world around them, although their attempts to do so often mean that they are incredibly busy. These executives often describe their organizations in terms of the broad and ever-expanding array of initiatives that they launch in an apparent effort to address each and every one of the opportunities and challenges emerging from change. It's hardly surprising that many of them are exhausted.

Provincial executives also tend to miss the big picture, quite possibly because they are concentrating so hard on small-scale details that they do not have the time or capacity to step back and look more widely. As a result, they frequently struggle to offer a coherent analysis of the critical themes underpinning the changes, and what these might mean for the future of the company – they have not pulled it all together. Blindness to the big picture both causes and exacerbates a focus on narrow, short-term thinking.

This in turn means that provincial executives appear to take an opportunistic approach to preparing for the future. They tend to use isolated changes as an opportunity to respond to immediate pressures and budgets, rather than consistently and systematically building their organization's readiness. Needless to say, provincial leaders can often be found in companies holding onto the past.

Let's take the hypothetical, although undoubtedly familiar, example of a CEO who is so involved in the minutiae of existing operations that he does not look at the bigger picture of what is happening around him. Unfortunately, his position as CEO means that he also decides what specific issues other executives in his organization should consider, which in turn limits their ability to look at the big picture, let alone take it into account. He leaves them no room for creativity or entrepreneurship because he sends out the message that hitting his targets is the top priority.

In many ways it is not surprising that so many leaders end up at or near this end of the spectrum. Many executives work long hours in stressful positions, and find it hard to make time for anything else, let alone for the reflection – about their firms and themselves – needed to prepare for the challenges to come. Some are very close to burnout; some have reached it. Even major companies have lost chief executives to overwork and exhaustion.

Pioneers At the other end of the leadership spectrum we encountered pioneers: men and women who are well informed about how the world is shifting around them and have perspectives on the future. They are genuinely curious, and always searching for more information: pioneers do not have the "I already know it all and there is nothing else you can tell me" attitude that can be found in some provincials. Our interviews with pioneers often ran considerably longer than planned simply because they were determined to see what they could learn from us at the same time as we were learning from them.

Pioneer executives are insightful about the implications of trends and global shifts for their markets, their businesses, and their organizations. They do not generally claim to have all the answers for the future, but they have thought through the issues, and are taking action in innovative and forward-looking ways.

This combination of focus, action, and a clear sense of direction can make them highly inspiring. They create a sense of excitement in their organizations, and use this to unleash the power in their people rather than to bolster their own position. Their biggest concern is keeping their organizations ahead of the game, which is doubtless why there is a clear correlation between pioneers and organizations which are actively preparing for the future.

How individuals lead their organization is clearly intertwined with, and shaped by, their personal attitude to leadership. Executives who feel personally and professionally overwhelmed by the challenges of the future are unlikely to feel that they should – or can – prepare their organization to meet them, and are far more likely to focus on comfortable short-term thinking. Those who feel well informed about the possibilities ahead are more likely to be taking innovative, inspirational approaches to preparing their organizations for the future.

Rethink your world

At the start of Rethink Your Playing Field we introduced the idea that it is impossible to prepare for the future without letting go of the past. The only way to understand the new reality being formed around us is by observing and analyzing it on its own terms. This logic applies to individuals just as much as it does to businesses and other organizations.

The personal challenges facing leaders are changing as the world around them changes. New generations are entering the workforce, bringing with them new ways of thinking. Multiple stakeholders now demand the attention that was once reserved for shareholders. Worldwide networks of connections are becoming ever more complex. Old approaches to leadership will not work in this new context; they must be replaced with a fresh approach based on what the world is becoming, not what it used to be.

This is why it is time for leaders to rethink their world, based on a fresh, clear-eyed look at their environment. A barrier to rethinking the world of the leader is once again the executive comfort zone, which discourages people from wanting even to attempt to change. Many leaders attribute their current success to having done things the right way in the past – and feel that they risk failure if they try to do things in any other way. In some cases, particularly as leaders become more senior, the comfort zone can manifest as a sort of arrogance: people feel that they have learnt all they need to in the past, and that they are now experienced enough just to get on with execution.

Nothing could be further from the truth. Constant learning is an essential foundation for leadership success in the future – as is a well thought-through personal purpose which we will discuss in the next section. And the correct starting point for the future is never what worked in the past, but what is needed for the future.

Challenging the role of the leader inside the organization

Some leaders see themselves as the center of their corporate universe, the guiding star in their organization. They see their actions and decisions as the reason for their firm's success, and believe that if they left, the business would not have a hope. They do not like sharing power. One CEO went so far as to say: "If the board doesn't like what I do and wants to interfere, it should just fire me and hire someone else."

Many such individuals tend to maintain a traditional, hierarchical approach to leadership, where they make decisions, and everyone else implements them. Typically they exhibit characteristics of the provincial approach and epitomize old style leadership. These individual leaders survive at all levels of many organizations.

One example of how this traditional behavior is reinforced is the common belief that new leaders have 100 days to prove themselves. The pressure that this creates for immediate, public action makes it very difficult for new leaders to be able to spend time learning about their organization and its challenges. Instead, they feel forced into quick decisions – which, with no time to develop new thinking tailored to the real situation, can result in them using old formulas for success in addressing any perceived problem. Such leaders can spend their careers 'solving' the problems they experienced at their last organization, rather than understanding and addressing those facing the company they have just joined. But these tradition-bound approaches to leadership will certainly not fit an organization that is trying to reshape how it works.

The changes we have described in earlier chapters highlight why individuals must rethink their understanding of what it means to be a leader. Future organizations will demand a different understanding of successful leadership. It is about support, inspiration, guidance, and encouragement. Leaders will no longer be expected to tell people what to do and how to do it, but to create the environment in which people are aligned behind the organization's purpose, and willing to put all their energy into achieving it.

They will be expected to understand that they are not the center of the corporate universe, and that other people also have much to offer. Leaders will need to learn how to develop others, to give them the space to think things through their own way, to take risks, to make mistakes – and to reward them for the courage it took to make them.

They need to be coach, mentor, teacher, even catalyst. Often they will need to lead from behind. Sometimes they will need to be in the middle. Sometimes they will need to brief their people and then remove themselves from the field of engagement entirely, trusting their team to deliver what is needed.

None of those things come naturally to provincial leaders, but they are the essence of pioneer leaders. Provincials are used to being in charge and ruling by right of formal authority; they find it difficult to make themselves vulnerable by trusting others. Nevertheless, those with the courage to make changes in their own behavior can make real progress towards becoming pioneers.

Take as an example the challenge described earlier in the book of moving from expecting employee loyalty to earning employee commitment. Expecting loyalty can be assigned as a task to others lower in the hierarchy, and tends to be managed using old-style tools such as employee compensation schemes.

However, when the focus shifts to building employee commitment, this approach will not work, because it takes more than the offer of a pay rise to earn commitment. Instead, leaders need to ask themselves a series of questions: Why would others want to join me in this organization's journey? How can I engage others in this journey? Why should the best people, who have many opportunities, choose to stay here? Am I offering them the opportunity to do work that allows them to have a meaningful impact?

Rethinking leadership inside the organization means asking these questions, then translating the answers into what it means for the roles, activities, and mindset of a leader.

Changing the role of the leader outside the organization

In many organizations, leaders, particularly those below the CEO, tend to focus closely on what happens within their part of the business, or to their bosses at more senior levels. This means that most executives keep their attention inside the business, generally aimed at what it is the people above them in the hierarchy want. As far as they are concerned, meeting the expectations of their boss is their top priority.

Senior leaders know that things are rather different. When they reach the top of the corporate pyramid, many described to us how they also become the very bottom of another. Suddenly they are responsible to a wide range of other people and stakeholders including the company's owners and the board that represents them; analysts and traders; governments and regulators; and consumers, NGOs, and society more broadly.

In other words, becoming a senior leader, even becoming CEO, does not mean unfettered power and control, but rather the acquisition of a whole new, and very different, set of bosses. This, combined with a future characterized by connections, creates very different challenges for leaders in their interactions outside their organization.

In this expanded role, leaders have to help their companies to negotiate a world with changing institutional roles, where they face growing uncertainty and volatility on all fronts – and where building connections is a critical part of preparing for the future. This is in contrast to the past, where many business leaders were not forced to look much beyond the borders of their firm or their industry unless they were actively seeking new opportunities. Their job was to do whatever was necessary to meet short-term internal targets , winning in their traditional industries against traditional competitors.

As connections become a new currency for organizational progress, and corporations start to be judged on long-term, sustainable success, this will have to change. Leaders will have to develop the ability to build relationships with outsiders, and to reflect the interests of the organization in the broader environment and the interests of the broader environment in their organization.

Looking beyond the recognized importance of emotional intelligence (EI), there are a new set of challenges for the leader. EI, popularized by Daniel Goleman, emphasizes the importance of leaders' self-awareness and self-management abilities – referred to as the personal domain – and the social awareness and social skills, in the social domain.[7] Looking ahead, it is likely that future leaders will need to take this thinking one step further as societal intelligence™ becomes an important extension to EI.

....

[7]   More information on the concept of emotional intelligence and the books on this subject by Daniel Goleman and others may be found at http://danielgoleman.info/

Societal intelligence is founded on an awareness of the needs of different stakeholder groups, and their interconnections and influence on the changing world.

It reflects an integrated perspective on the relationship between business and society, applied not only to relationship management, but to an organization's impact on society, and the search for mutual benefits and value creation.

Societally intelligent leaders reshape their organizations so that continued growth does not increase their impact on the environment. They also seek out investors who are more interested in long-term, sustainable success than in short-term profits which allows them to align the company's ownership base behind its long-term vision. Such businesses and leaders have a holistic view of their impact on society beyond the direct activities of the firm, for example the impact through their extended networks, including consumers and suppliers. The most advanced in this type of thinking also encourage others to take up the challenge of creating mutual benefits with society, beyond just delivering the bottom line.

Thinking beyond work-life balance

Most, if not all, executives with whom we spoke described the need to reevaluate where and how they spend their time; most are so busy that they could spend all their waking hours working, if they so chose.

They should not, however, base this reevaluation on an outdated view of work-life balance. More often today work and life are not seen as separate and distinct, where people need to make an either-or choice between a well-grounded, enjoyable life, and a successful career.

Rather leaders describe the need to ask a different question: How can people integrate their lives and work in a way that allows them to improve all aspects? Leaders learn lessons from outside their workplace that help them to develop how they operate within it, and vice versa. Successful leadership means reexamining not simply how you divide your time and effort between different activities, but how you can use them all to enable and reinforce one another. It is impossible for leaders to rethink the world without looking at their entire world, not just the part they see while they are wearing a suit or sitting in an office.

Rethinking this holistically can be challenging. Many – perhaps most – executives compartmentalize their lives. They work at the office, they contribute to society by volunteering with a local charity, they deal with their spiritual needs at church or temple, and so on. But as long as people segment themselves like this, they will never reach their potential. Instead of having bridges between the different aspects so that energy can be shared, they end up trying to run several lives, each of which compete for time and attention. This is a huge drain of energy and concentration: leaders sit in meetings at work worrying that they are missing a school play, and spend their time at the gym checking emails on their BlackBerry, for example. No activity gets the attention it deserves. In the worst-case scenario, it's almost like trying to control multiple personalities.

Leaders need to bring all parts of themselves to work if they want all their resources at their disposal. This means that they need to develop a high degree of self-awareness and a connection to their sense of higher purpose, or risk imploding. People who take a holistic approach to life that keeps all parts in balance, rather than in competition, will be more at ease with themselves, and thus more approachable to those around them. They also need to take the lessons and experience from their work to their outside life again to bring their full selves to everything they do.

This integrated approach will put them in a much better position to digest and incorporate information from all the different things that they do, providing them with much broader and richer perspectives on how the world – and the people within it – are changing. Organizations need to rethink their playing field without traditional industry boundaries because their competitors no longer look like they do. Similarly, individual leaders need to integrate their lives into one complete whole to spot connections growing in the world around them, and make sense of the burgeoning mountain of information they receive.

Having an open mind about what can be learned from all these different places will also give leaders more time to reflect, because every skill that they learn contributes to all aspects of their lives – old-style boundaries that insist that skills developed during a hobby are meaningless at the office, for example, are no longer relevant.

Building and leading an integrated life is important but not easy, as Clara Gaymard told us when we asked how she coped with running GE France while looking after nine children. "There is no easy life," she said. "But what I would say is that all the things you experience in your personal life give you training and values for your business life. So it's not a question of managing. And it's not a question of separating personal life and professional life. It is all one. You are connected all the time."

Ask yourself: have you rethought your world?

Old notions of what it means to be a leader, and how you can get the most from your people, are becoming outdated. Future-ready organizations need to be led by men and women who have rethought their own roles in the context of the changes around us.

Ask yourself:

Leadership What is your role as a leader in your organization today? Are you ready to take on the challenge of building trust and commitment among your people, even if it means working through influence rather than power?

Relationships Have you identified the key stakeholders with whom you need to build and maintain relationships outside your organization? Do you have the skills needed to do this?

Integration Have you integrated the different aspects of your life? Do you focus on giving each aspect enough quality time? Are you learning from each aspect, and connecting those insights into a whole?

• •

Redefine your ambition as a leader, and as a person

Not only must leaders preparing for the future rethink their world, they must also clarify and redefine their personal ambition and purpose.

Keeping busy is easy. It's not just organizations infected with the curse of confusing activity with purpose; individuals, too, are doing more than ever before. Executives take on more tasks than time allows. They are constantly fire-fighting in an attempt to keep short-term pressures at bay just a little longer. They become exhausted, overstretched, and, just like organizations, they struggle to get off the busyness treadmill long enough to make real change, let alone ask themselves a few searching questions: Is this activity getting me anywhere? Do I even know where I want to go?

Too often the answer to both of these questions, if they were asked, would be no.

This is why leaders need to redefine their personal ambition so that they have a clear purpose and vision to guide their decision-making, just as organizations do. This will help them work out how they can learn from the past rather than holding on to it, and how they can help shape the future they want, rather than simply reacting as circumstances change, and change again.

Two-directional thinking is as important for redefining individual ambition as it is for companies. Leaders need to decide what matters to them, what they want to achieve, and how they need to shape their decisions now to work forward from the present and back from their planned goal to achieve it.

Part of redefining the ambition of a firm is developing a meaningful purpose, which requires thinking more widely about the stakeholders to whom a company is responsible, and just what those responsibilities are. The end result is often that businesses become more thoughtful and more involved with society as a whole.

Such changes have implications for leaders too. As lives become less compartmentalized and the structures which gave them shape disappear, it is more important than ever that individuals have a clear sense of personal purpose to guide them through life. When this purpose is aligned with that of their employer, people find it easier to lead through inspiration and influence, rather than hierarchical power. A clear, aligned personal and professional purpose also offers practical help, as it makes it easier for leaders to decide which activities will help an organization achieve its purpose, and which are irrelevant to it.

This can be seen in the way Peter Bakker used his personal purpose – "saving the world" – in his leadership of TNT, the logistics business. Bakker, who is now president of the World Business Council for Sustainable Development, used his personal purpose to guide him when rethinking the business's playing field. He realized that TNT's logistical capabilities, combined with its geographic reach, would put it in a good position to assist with food distribution after an earthquake, tsunami, or other natural disaster. He went on to sign an agreement with the World Food Program to this effect, and trained 100 people in the company's Dutch office to be part of emergency teams that can be flown to disaster zones at short notice.

While there are strong parallels between redefining organizational and individual purpose, in the latter case it might be more accurate to speak of defining rather than redefining. Our research suggests that very few people have thought about their personal purpose or values, and even among those who have done so, unlike Bakker, many seem unable to articulate their position clearly and simply, which is what gives a purpose real power.

Many leaders discover their sense of purpose after some sort of defining moment in their lives: the arrival of a child or a serious illness, for example. Such important life events trigger a thinking process that makes leaders more conscious about what they do and why they do it. But such an event is not a necessity. Individuals who want to redefine (or define) their values simply need to find the time and space for reflection. We offer suggestions on how to do this later in this chapter.

You have to know yourself to show yourself

"Authentic leadership" has become a cliché of management literature – unfairly so. Authenticity simply means that people need to know themselves, and need to be prepared to show that self to others. It means individuals understanding what they want out of life, and acting accordingly.

Understanding, articulating, and living in line with your personal purpose is a strong foundation for building stronger, more genuine relationships inside and outside an organization. It enhances an individual's ability to influence and inspire others. Leaders who articulate their principles clearly, and follow them consistently, will find that employees are more willing to accept their decisions because the logic driving them is much more transparent. This degree of positive predictability can provide an important element of stability as workforces come to terms with the dissolution of the bureaucracy that used to provide security.

A genuine purpose will also help to avoid the sort of staged authenticity that has given the word its poor reputation. Leaders can try to create the appearance of authenticity in all sorts of ways, but when the fake is spotted, the leader's reputation and his or her message will both be damaged.

Note that, just as in our discussions of purpose and organization, contrasting an investment bank's purpose to that of the Mahindra Group, it also holds that personal purpose will clarify and define the expectations of others in their interactions and in their relationship.

• •

Perspectives from the front line: purpose

Leo Yip *"When you see leaders acting or deciding inconsistently, I sometimes think it is because their authenticity is not there,"* the chairman of Singapore's Economic Development Board told us. *"Over time, their people will see through that. They will want to know who their leaders truly are.*

"Who you are as a leader is based on your sense of purpose, values, and everything else about you. These things have to be consistently translated into your decisions, your actions, your priorities, and who you are as people interact with you. Only then can you build trust. Without trust, you cannot have leadership. Without trust, you can only have some following some of the time, but it's not true leadership."

Feike Sijbesma The CEO of DSM's personal purpose came into focus when he thought about the world that his two sons and all other children will inherit; he said: this was his responsibility too, he decided, to improve it.

"I feel a little bit like, 'Hey, we run a company here. We are in a society here. We are a part of society, and we need to take care of the next generations, those who will live here after us,'" he told us. *"I cannot say to my two boys, 'Well, we had a good life, but the problems we created are all yours.'*

This insight into what mattered to him as an individual has helped him to shape not just the decisions that he makes as a leader – for example, around repositioning the former chemical company now as a life sciences and materials sciences business that can help solve social and environmental issues – but how he leads. He has seen that the next generations think and act differently from those that went before them, and that anyone who hopes to lead them will need to adapt accordingly.

Anand Mahindra The Mahindra Group's chairman highlighted the importance of personal transparency and purpose in engaging an organization. *"When you tell people to work according to a transcending goal, to do something more than coming in to work for the next quarter's earnings, they carry you. It's not like taking a rope and pulling an iron horse behind you. It's more like there's this wonderful surf coming behind you that's just carrying you along and keeping you on top of the wave. You don't have to sweat an inch. You just have to walk the talk, and you have to smell honest.*

"The first thing a CEO has to understand is that you can't con people. You know the saying: 'You can con some people some of the time, but not all the people all the time.' Even that's wrong. I don't think you can con anyone any part of the time. That's a little bit arrogant. People understand when somebody really believes what he or she says, and they really mean what they say, and if you're true to yourself and to this objective you set up, you will just get swept along with that tide. It is a movement of a kind."

Robert Polet Knowing and sharing your purpose makes leadership easier, said the former CEO of the Gucci Group. *"Working at Gucci, I've been allowed to be me. Nobody tried to force anything on me, or say 'You have to do this.' And the purpose in life, I think, has to be to try to capitalize on those things that you do really well, to develop yourself and utilize all of your skills, while staying completely in charge of your own destiny.*

"You are the only one who is responsible for yourself, nobody else. And if you don't accept who you are, if you are holding back all the time, then you can't be true to yourself. You can't be good, you can't be a good partner for anybody else, whether that is your wife, your kids, or the people who are working for you."

• •

Ask yourself: have you redefined your ambition?

A clear purpose and a moral compass will help you make decisions that are both consistent and authentic.

Ask yourself:

Purpose How do you define success in your life? What legacy do you want to leave behind? What impact do you want to have on the world, on your business, and on your family?

Values What are your core values and principles that shape how you think and behave every day? What else do you need to do to clarify your values, and act in accordance with them?

• •

Reshape how you live, lead, and connect

Just as with organizations, rethinking your world and redefining your ambition and purpose are necessary steps to take in preparing for the future. However, until concrete actions are taken to change it is all largely a nice intellectual exercise.

Let's now assume that you have taken the time to rethink your world, including the challenges of being a leader inside and outside of your work. You have developed a point of view on how your world as a leader and as a person will change in the future. Let's also assume that you redefined your ambition, not just in terms of short-term success but also in the long term. Now the challenge is bringing this understanding and clarity into everyday life.

Developing an honest understanding of the world and a clear view of what you want to achieve in it is difficult. The next stage is harder still: taking – and keeping – control of your own agenda. Executives who do not define and articulate their own agenda will become victims of others' agendas.

In the final section on the 3Rs of preparing yourself for the future, we share a number of pieces of advice and practical tools suggested by the leaders we met, all of whom are also struggling with these issues. Some will be more relevant when rethinking, others when redefining, but we have brought them together here because leaders need to reshape their lives so that they can make these changes.

Below we describe eight areas that were frequently raised in our interviews: make time for reflection and regeneration; control your own agenda; build personal relationships with stakeholders; personally tap into the power of diversity; embrace challenge as a gift, not a threat; focus on enabling others to succeed; be prepared to take a stand; learn from the past, prepare for the future, live in the present.

1. Make time for reflection and regeneration

All change requires thought and preparation, and all meaningful thought requires time and space for reflection. Leaders cannot rethink their worlds or define their personal purpose when they are under siege from the demands of day-to-day life. In fact, few leaders can perform at their best even in day-to-day tasks without the occasional opportunity to regenerate, reenergize, and take stock of where they are.

Peggy Dulany, the chairman of the Synergos Institute, puts it very simply. "Unless the leaders of today and tomorrow are self-aware individuals, and connected to themselves and their sense of higher purpose, they're probably at some point going to implode, or at least be much less effective as they move forward," she told us. "Life is stressful, and there is so much more to do than any individual possibly can."

While most leaders we spoke with valued having time to reflect and regenerate, not all saw it as important. One told us it was a "rubbish question": he did not need time to reflect, because he already knew what he was doing. Another told us that the real issue was execution. "There is always enough time to think because you are sitting in planes and waiting for meetings," he said. "It sounds a bit arrogant, but I think the issue is not time to think, but rather time to make sure that things get done." Unfortunately such attitudes are all too common, and can be a barrier to preparing both the individual and the organization for the future.

The extreme busyness facing most leaders does not make it easy for people to step away from their day-to-day lives. Taking that step is, however, necessary. It is by far the most effective way for people to reconnect with themselves, clarify what it is they want to achieve – rather than letting this be shaped by others around them – and create the solid foundation on which to build their own personal futures.

Time away from the constant barrage of short-term demands is critical for leaders who want to develop clarity and insight that will let them shape a new way of leading for the future, rather than holding on to outdated approaches.

How you use this time can vary. It does not have to be spent in silent contemplation of the future, although that has its place; it can be any pursuit that frees your mind to think about what you want, and about who you are. Some people play sport. Some read, or act, or spend time walking along the beach enjoying nature. We met one CEO who practices yoga for an hour before work every morning.

The important thing is that the activity allows you to create enough distance from the immediate issues facing you to be able to look at them, and your life more broadly, in a holistic manner. Your goal should be to develop a clearer perspective of your personal strengths and how you can use them to address these issues without slipping into autopilot.

2. Control your own agenda

Create and control your own agenda. If you don't, you will likely become the victim of the agendas of others: it's that simple.

If you want to see just how much of your life is controlled by others, you should look at how much time you spend on activities that you consider to add value; everything you do that does not add value is there because someone else is controlling what you do and how you do it.

Your agenda should focus on what you want to achieve, and should let you allocate time and effort to the activities you consider important. Rethinking your world and defining your ambition will help you to clarify your priorities, but it is only by reshaping how you lead that you will be able to put them in to practice.

The first step is accepting that "they" cannot stop you. Too often leaders have good intentions, but fail to put them in to practice because "they" won't let them do it or "they" won't give them time. This is nothing but an excuse, and a poor one at that. You are a leader. If you allow others to dominate your agenda and your time, you are a victim of the very system you are meant to be leading.

Having your own agenda enables clarifying and shaping your priorities. It makes it easy to see whether or not a particular task or project or activity contributes to those priorities. It is easier to say no to non-value adding tasks or requests when you are clear on where you want to spend your time, and what the benefits are of doing so. Then it is simply a matter of saying no to anything that does not. And make time to review your diary or schedule regularly so that you can cross out activities that are added to it but which are not directly associated with your priorities.

3. Build personal relationships with stakeholders

It is not just companies that need to move from transactional to collaborative relationships. Leaders, too, need to find a way to build personal relationships with external stakeholders, and not just the friendly ones. You need to have dialogs that allow mutual understanding and influence. If you cannot do this at an individual level, it is likely that your company will struggle to do so at an organizational level. In a connected future, all connections matter.

Dialogs and relationships are critical because they offer the potential for personal and organizational impact. And by dialogs here we do not mean the defending, selling, or pretending to listen dialogs we described in the last chapter, but rather the ones that can contribute to understanding and co-creating solutions.

Think back to the inverted pyramid that a new leader joins. One implication of the leader's role in this new pyramid is that you now have the authority to speak out publicly on issues, beyond just the firm's profit margin, that matter to your organization and to you personally.

The importance of connections does not mean that you have to have relationships with everybody about everything. Rather, you need to use your view on the future, your organization's purpose, and your own agenda to focus on the relationships that matter.

Note that these may not always be the obvious relationships. "It is important that you explore the periphery of your network," Peggy Dulany told us. "It is important that you try to understand why something's not working, and explore why. This is the source of important new insight." In this process, she also added on the importance of trust: "Chains of trust are what lead to the possibility of working together."

4. Personally tap into the power of diversity

Many leaders talk a good game when it comes to diversity, but rather fewer put it in to practice in their own world, particularly at senior levels in organizations. Look at the team around you: Is it genuinely diverse? If not, why not? If diversity is important for others, it is also important for you.

Diversity is not simply a question of gender, nationality, or ethnicity. In its broadest, truest sense it is about different ways of thinking, and so encompasses all the differences above and many more, including functions and professions. You need to grasp its potential because it will help challenge your thinking and build your understanding, and it will also help your organization to attract and engage with the best individuals, to tap into the new insights that different mindsets make possible, and thus to better understand and prepare for the future.

Unfortunately individual leaders' assumptions and preconceptions can create barriers to diversity. A common excuse made by leaders with few senior women at their organization is that it takes more time to develop them, for example. Do not fall into the same trap. And do not assume that launching initiatives will solve the problem, either; leaders must take a visible, personal stance to embrace it.

5. Embrace challenge as a gift

Leadership can be lonely. The more senior leaders become, the lonelier it gets.

Many hierarchical leaders feel that they are expected to know all the answers; that their role is to exude strength, confidence, and certainty. This leaves them little room to test new ideas or explore possibilities, because any such behavior could be seen as demonstrating uncertainty or indecisiveness.

But organizations of the future will not be led by generals. They will be led by men and women who can create an environment in which everyone's voice can be heard, everyone's insights are valued. Doing this means being open to challenge – indeed, embracing it. This sort of environment can reinforce preparations for the future by encouraging people to speak up when they see old mindsets or old attitudes holding the company in the past – even if the person holding that mindset is their boss.

Developing this openness can be personally confronting. It requires you to seek out challenge, allow vulnerability, listen to others, and focus on what is best for your organization rather than on protecting your own position. Surrounding yourself with a diverse, empowered, and accountable team of trusted colleagues is a good place to start. From there, begin seeking challenge from people whose perspectives are fundamentally different to your own.

6. Focus on enabling others to succeed

The first response when we asked leaders about their main challenges for the future was almost always "people." It was almost a platitude, which became more obvious when probing what they mean by people, how they develop these people, and how they need to personally engage with this issue. Here the answers were typically much less clear.

A central feature that we have suggested in the changing role of the leader is a shift from viewing their role as primarily that of a decision-maker and manager of activities to creator of the environment in which others can succeed. In a future characterized by uncertainty, volatility and complexity, the ability to tap into the collective strengths and "intelligence" of the entire organization is critical for success.

Many leaders find developing and trusting others the hardest aspect of their job. It is also the most important. And this importance will only increase: in the future tapping into the collective strengths and knowledge of the entire organization is critical. Leaders will only be successful if they enable others to succeed.

Accepting this new definition of leadership success is a big step in the right direction. Doing this means putting aside old ideas that it can be measured in the number of deals closed or investments made.

Enabling others to succeed does not mean ignoring shortcomings. In fact, in some circumstances the best way to enable others' success is to get rid of your leadership team, and building a new one from scratch.

Dick Boer, the CEO of Ahold, described coming to this realization as a turning point in his leadership. "It was at that moment that I thought, okay, the only change I can make is getting the leadership around me which has the same culture and strategy as I believe in," he said. "In all my previous cases, it had always been possible to influence it easily, to change it, but it was hard to do that here.

"So, in 2003 I changed the whole management team in a couple of months. I lost some I didn't want to lose, but some of the losses were really necessary. Then I created a complete new leadership team, with a new structure, with a new hands-on mentality, with a different culture – people who understood that you have to engage your organization instead of telling them their roles and the way they have to work.

"You come back to yourself, and this was not me. I was running a company in a way I didn't want. I didn't want to have to leave, I wanted to change it. I wanted a team I could trust to do things, who had the same goals and values I did, not one where I had to control everybody for the whole day."

Enabling the success of others applies equally outside the organization. As stakeholder relationships move from being transactional to collaborative, your role as a leader will include accountability for the success of those key stakeholders with whom you interact.

7. Be prepared to take a stand

Blaming others for your organization's failings – or those of your business unit or function – does not help anyone. As one leader put it: "If every time the idiot is the predecessor and the potential successors, maybe the issue is the one in between."

Leaders at all levels must be prepared to face reality and to stand up for what they believe in, even if such beliefs are unfashionable or unpopular. This is the most meaningful way to demonstrate both transparency and consistency, and an important step in gaining the trust of those around you.

Many organizations are waiting for leaders to step forward and guide the organization in looking to the future. But doing this requires you to step beyond day-to-day issues, to be willing to put forward your aspirations for the organization and to inspire others to join the journey. This challenge exists for leaders at all levels of organizations.

Taking on this role requires personal transparency and trust. If you are not transparent yourself, how can you expect others to be? Transparency and courage are critical in building trust, which is the foundation for even the possibility of working together.

As you prepare for the future, you must be clear on what you stand for, be willing to put forward these key beliefs and ambitions, and invite others to engage in the journey moving forward.

8. Learn from the past, prepare for the future, live in the present

If you want to be able to let go of the past, you need to be able to learn from it. The key is reflecting on the past, not attempting to repeat it. Lessons from the past can be drawn from the tools that you have used, and what these can accomplish; the challenges that you and your organization have faced, and what changes were needed to respond; and from the personal lessons and experiences that have shaped your individual purpose. Being too busy today to reflect back is not an acceptable excuse. Readiness for the future is built on the foundations of the past.

Earlier in this chapter we discussed provincials and pioneers. At the provincial end of the leadership spectrum we saw individuals who were overwhelmed by change, oblivious to the big picture, and opportunistic about how they approached the future. At the other end we saw pioneers: people who were informed, insightful, and inspirational in leading their organizations toward the future. Making the time to work towards becoming a pioneer is critical.

It is easy to get so caught up in the demands of today and the agendas of others that you feel too busy to make the time for reflection, but this tendency must be resisted. This is where having spent the time clarifying your ambition and your purpose, and focusing on the dual challenges of delivering results today and investing for the future, come together. This is why it is essential to live, lead, and connect in the present.

Operating in this complex, changing world requires you to be grounded at each moment of each day so that you can make the right choices, ask the right questions, engage and listen to the right people, and respond to the immediate. Remember, the challenge of preparing for the future is not how to ignore the present and its short-term pressures, but how to develop the capacity to prepare for the long term while still delivering results today. It requires building an agenda and way of leading and living that integrates these two challenges into a single integrated whole. You must be able to live in both worlds, and recognize what this means for each day.

Ask yourself: have you reshaped your leadership?

Preparing yourself to lead means changing what you do and how you do it, not just how you think about your role.

Ask yourself:

Time Have you create space in your day to think, rethink, and reflect?

Transparency Are you honest and open with others about your emotions, motivations, and values? Do you know yourself and do you show yourself?

Challenge Do you encourage challenge, even when it is personally confronting?

Relationships Have you built connections with all stakeholders, including those outside your organization? Have you found an effective way to select, build, and motivate your team?

Culture Have you created an environment that will prepare your organization to change?

Readiness Are you taking steps to stay healthy, mentally and physically? Are you open to constant learning?

Flexibility Do you adapt your leadership style to different circumstances?

• •

Embarking on the journey

We are living through a period of unprecedented challenge. It is also a time of unprecedented opportunity. How you view it will depend on how you approach your role as a leader.

Many leaders we spoke with view the change we are seeing today as truly the opportunity of a lifetime. Leaders can embrace the new definition of success in the future and, in doing so, take responsibility for improving not just their organization, but the world around us. They can – you can – find ways to address challenges facing business while helping society, and vice versa. You can change the lives of countless individuals, both inside and outside your organization. You can develop yourself, and your role, in ways that allow you to understand and fulfill your purpose.

Making the most of these opportunities will take preparation and commitment.

All of the inspirational CEOs and leaders we had the pleasure of interacting with recognized this opportunity and this responsibility. They were inquisitive. They were concerned about the institutions that they led and the people they affected. They wanted their legacy to be a positive impact on the world.

This book was written to help you prepare yourself and your organization for the future by helping you understand the challenges and opportunities ahead. It was written not to provide answers or a formula for success, it was written to help guide you on the journey to understand these opportunities and challenges so that you can make the choices of how you will do this yourself. All three of us authors of this book have confidence in individuals to make the right choices for themselves and their organizations if they can be supported in asking the right questions. Here we sincerely hope that we have provided at least some questions to aid you in this process.

The day you as an individual stop learning, stop exploring, stop challenging and stop connecting is the day you stop leading. Enjoy the journey.

Five principles of personal readiness

1. You must stay at the forefront of any change that you wish to create in an organization.

2. There is no "they" in leadership. "They won't let us" is an unacceptable excuse: you must take responsibility for finding a way to do what must be done.

3. You may be at the top of the organizational pyramid, but you are at the bottom when it comes to the world in which your organization operates. This is why you must broaden your role, influence, and impact outside the organization.

4. Leadership is not about personal power. It is about facilitating, focusing, and enabling the power of others. Engagement, collaboration, and commitment are essential leadership tools.

5. The day that you stop learning is the day that you stop leading. Reflection, challenge, and regeneration are critical for every leader.

APPENDIX: Information about the research

Our research set out to investigate how top leaders – mainly in businesses, but also from other organizations – saw the challenges and opportunities facing the world in which they operate, the institutions that they led, and themselves as leaders looking five to 10 years in the future. The questions we asked focused first on how these individuals saw these challenges and opportunities looking forward, then on the actions that they were taking today to prepare their businesses, their organizations and, importantly, themselves for this future.

The research involved face-to-face interviews with 156 CEOs or other top leaders from around the world. While we originally started by interviewing 50 CEOs, our first analysis of this data suggested that there were differences in the patterns of views held leaders of developed world businesses compared with those based in rapidly-developing economies – the BRICS and beyond. We therefore widened the study to test these hypotheses and to ensure a sufficient sample size.

Table 1 provides an overview of the companies and individuals interviewed. For individuals, the table offers a summary of their positions at the time of the interviews, as well as their gender. For organizations, the table provides information on the location of each company's headquarters. Table 2 lists the industries represented by organizations included in the study, while Table 3 lists the different ownership structures of the organizations. Our intention in the research was to maximize diversity across all of these variables as thoroughly as possible, given constraints around ability to access the individuals, in order to look for trends and patterns that could be generalized. The interviews were conducted between 2009 and 2012.

The interviews employed a semi-structured format based around the topics and questions outlined in Table 4. All interviews were recorded and transcribed, with interviews subsequently being coded by two coders and analysed using Nvivo (software that supports analysis of qualitative and mixed methods research) to identify patterns and trends.

Each interview lasted between one and two and a half hours. At the beginning many individuals often asked if we could complete the interview faster than scheduled, as they were busy. In a majority of these instances, however, the interviews actually ran over the allotted time. In considering why this happened we discovered that many leaders are actively struggling with the issues we are addressing and none have as yet found all the answers to how to prepare their organizations and themselves today for the future. Most leaders saw challenges in better understanding how the world is changing and how can they move beyond the short-term, financially driven strategic plans that shape many businesses' regular routines and thinking.

Despite recent waves of corporate scandals and negative press about CEO arrogance, we were pleasantly surprised by the passion, belief, and vision of many of the leaders we interviewed. Even with all the daily pressures to deliver in the short term, there was a strong desire to actively prepare for the future. However, there were some self-interested individuals that still clung to the belief that the sole role of business, and their role as leader, was to ensure short-term profit maximization. Fortunately, these were in a minority, potentially influenced by our sample.

The focus of this research and this book is to share the wisdom, experience, and insights of the many leaders we had the opportunity and privilege of interviewing in order to challenge current and future leaders on what it will take to be successful in the future. Our intention in this book is both to provide insights about the issues of preparing for the future today, and to challenge the thinking of leaders about what they must individually and collectively do to prepare themselves and their institutions.

Table 1: Interviews

Position (at time of interview)	Number
Chairman, CEO, President	136
Other	20

Gender	Number
Male	139
Female	17

Headquarters location	Number
United States	15
Europe	59
Brazil/Latin America	19
China	10
India	11
Other Asia	30
South Africa	12

Table 2: Industries represented in the research

Conglomerates
Fast-moving consumer goods (FMCG)
Banking and finance
Light industry
Shipping/logistics
Retailing
Media
Advertising
NGOs

Table 3: Ownership structures represented in the research

Public
Family
Family/public
State-owned
NGO/other

Table 4: Interview topics (Semi-structured questionnaire guide)

Topics	Question areas
General questions	1. What are the biggest opportunities and challenges facing the world over the next 5-10 year period? 2. What are the biggest opportunities and challenges facing your organization over the next 5-10 year period? 3. What are the biggest personal challenges facing you as a leader over the next 5-10 years?
Where are you leading your organization	1. How would you define success for your organization in 5-10 years? 2. How will your organization be different 5-10 years from now? 3. What are the major dilemma's, trade-offs or paradoxes your face as you lead your organization toward this direction? 4. What are the major leadership challenges you face in setting and managing the direction in which you lead your organization? 5. What role do values play in your organization today? How do you expect this to change looking forward? 6. How are you influenced by stakeholders today? How do you expect this to change in the future? 7. How do you balance your focus on short- and long-term issues? How is this changing looking forward?
How are your relationships changing as you prepare for the future	1. How do you see your relationships between your organization and consumers changing? ...customers? ...suppliers? ...employees? ...other stakeholders? ...society? ...owners and shareholders? ...your board? 2. What are you doing to prepare your organization for these changing relationships?
Personal leadership stories	1. Share an experience or story about when you were at your best as a leader. 2. Share an experience of story about where you were out of control as a leader, a negative experience. 3. What lessons and impact did these stories have on your leadership?
Future leaders	1. How will your successor need to be different from you in terms of how they lead the business? 2. What advice do you give to high potential leaders in your organization? 3. When promoting or hiring a senior leader, what criteria to you apply in assessing an individual? 4. How do you manage diversity in your senior leadership? 5. What do you think it will take to be a great leader in the future? 6. Who are 2-3 leaders you admire the most? Why?
Self	1. Where do you get your energy from as a leader? 2. What role do work-life issues play in how your approach your job and your personal life? 3. What do you consider to be your personal strengths and weaknesses as a leader?

ABOUT THE AUTHORS

Thomas W. Malnight is Professor of Strategy at the International Institute for Management Development (IMD) in Lausanne Switzerland. Among other work, Tom is the co-author of Must Win Battles: How to Win Them Again and Again. Previously Tom was on the Faculty of the Wharton School of the University of Pennsylvania and has a DBA from the Harvard Business School and an MBA from the Wharton School.

He works extensively with top leadership teams in challenging how they view their changing competitive landscape, how they shape their future and strategies for moving forward, how they engage and align priorities and actions across their organizations, and how they work together as a focused high performing leadership team.

Tracey S. Keys is a Director of Strategy Dynamics Global SA, publisher of www.globaltrends.com. Prior to founding Strategy Dynamics Global SA, Tracey worked with senior executives at IMD, and has held senior roles at the BBC, Booz &Co., Deloitte & Touche and Braxton Associates, as well as being an active advisor to a number of start-ups. Tracey is a Fulbright Scholar and holds an MBA from The Wharton School, University of Pennsylvania where she was distinguished as a Palmer Scholar. She is also a co-author of Must-Win Battles, and co-editor of Mastering Executive Education: How to Combine Content With Context and Emotion.

She works with senior executives and leadership teams globally on complex issues of strategy, preparing organizations for the future, and developing perspectives on global trends, as well as engaging in public speaking on these topics, and consulting on executive education programs.

ABOUT THE AUTHORS

Kees van der Graaf In 2008, at the pinnacle of his career, Kees decided to take early retirement from consumer goods giant, Unilever. His career there spanned over 30 years, culminating as the President of Europe and a member of the Board and Executive Committee. During his final years at Unilever, he completely overhauled the European business and brought it back to growth.

Since retiring, in addition to spending time with his family, Kees' top priority is to support the FSHD Foundation, which he and his wife Renée founded in the hopes of finding a cure for FSHD. Kees also spends a significant amount of time at IMD, where he was an Executive-in-Residence from 2008 until 2012. He serves on several boards, engages in public speaking, and through his consultancy – Los Gravos BV – advises organizations, including many international fast-moving consumer goods firms on complexity management. All of Kees' activities are aimed at raising funds for FSHD Research.

OTHER BOOKS BY THE AUTHORS

The Global Trends Report 2013
Thomas W. Malnight and Tracey S. Keys
Published by Strategy Dynamics Global SA, 2012

Must-Win Battles: How to Win Them Again and Again
Peter Killing and Thomas Malnight with Tracey Keys
Published by Financial Times Prentice Hall/Wharton School Publishing, 2005

Defining Moments: What Every Leader Should Know About Balancing Life
Kees van der Graaf
Published by IMD, 2011

19364148R00113

Made in the USA
Middletown, DE
16 April 2015